Git Pocket Guide

Richard E. Silverman

Beijing · Cambridge · Farnham · Köln · Sebastopol · Tokyo

Git Pocket Guide

by Richard E. Silverman

Copyright © 2013 Richard E. Silverman. All rights reserved.

Printed in the United States of America.

Published by O'Reilly Media, Inc., 1005 Gravenstein Highway North, Sebastopol, CA 95472.

O'Reilly books may be purchased for educational, business, or sales promotional use. Online editions are also available for most titles (*http://my.safaribooksonline.com*). For more information, contact our corporate/institutional sales department: 800-998-9938 or *corporate@oreilly.com*.

Editors: Mike Loukides and Meghan Blanchette
Production Editor: Melanie Yarbrough
Copyeditor: Kiel Van Horn
Proofreader: Linley Dolby
Indexer: Judith McConville
Cover Designer: Randy Comer
Interior Designer: David Futato
Illustrator: Rebecca Demarest

June 2013:   First Edition

Revision History for the First Edition:

2013-06-24:	First release
2013-07-10:	Second release
2013-08-30:	Third release

See *http://oreilly.com/catalog/errata.csp?isbn=9781449325862* for release details.

Nutshell Handbook, the Nutshell Handbook logo, and the O'Reilly logo are registered trademarks of O'Reilly Media, Inc. *Git Pocket Guide*, the image of a long-eared bat, and related trade dress are trademarks of O'Reilly Media, Inc.

Many of the designations used by manufacturers and sellers to distinguish their products are claimed as trademarks. Where those designations appear in this book, and O'Reilly Media, Inc., was aware of a trademark claim, the designations have been printed in caps or initial caps.

ISBN: 978-1-449-32586-2

[LSI]

Table of Contents

Preface

What Is Git?

Git is a tool for tracking changes made to a set of files over time, a task traditionally known as "version control." Although it is most often used by programmers to coordinate changes to software source code, and it is especially good at that, you can use Git to track any kind of content at all. Any body of related files evolving over time, which we'll call a "project," is a candidate for using Git. With Git, you can:

- Examine the state of your project at earlier points in time

- Show the differences among various states of the project

- Split the project development into multiple independent lines, called "branches," which can evolve separately

- Periodically recombine branches in a process called "merging," reconciling the changes made in two or more branches

- Allow many people to work on a project simultaneously, sharing and combining their work as needed

…and much more.

There have been many different version control systems developed in the computing world, including SCCS, RCS, CVS,

Subversion, BitKeeper, Mercurial, Bazaar, Darcs, and others. Some particular strengths of Git are:

- Git is a member of the newer generation of *distributed* version control systems. Older systems such as CVS and Subversion are *centralized*, meaning that there is a single, central copy of the project content and history to which all users must refer. Typically accessed over a network, if the central copy is unavailable for some reason, all users are stuck; they cannot use version control until the central copy is working again. Distributed systems such as Git, on the other hand, have no inherent central copy. Each user has a complete, independent copy of the entire project history, called a "repository," and full access to all version control facilities. Network access is only needed occasionally, to share sets of changes among people working on the same project.

- In some systems, notably CVS and Subversion, branches are slow and difficult to use in practice, which discourages their use. Branches in Git, on the other hand, are very fast and easy to use. Effective branching and merging allows more people to work on a project in parallel, relying on Git to combine their separate contributions.

- Applying changes to a repository is a two-step process: you add the changes to a staging area called the "index," then commit those changes to the repository. The extra step allows you to easily apply just some of the changes in your current working files (including a subset of changes to a single file), rather than being forced to apply them all at once, or undoing some of those changes yourself before committing and then redoing them by hand. This encourages splitting changes up into better organized, more coherent and reusable sets.

- Git's distributed nature and flexibility allow for many different styles of use, or "workflows." Individuals can share work directly between their personal repositories. Groups can coordinate their work through a single central repository. Hybrid schemes permit several people to organize the contributions of others to different areas of a project, and then collaborate among themselves to maintain the overall project state.

- Git is the technology behind the enormously popular "social coding" website GitHub (*http://github.com/*), which includes many well-known open source projects. In learning Git, you will open up a whole world of collaboration on small and large scales.

Goals of This Book

There are already several good books available on Git, including Scott Chacon's *Pro Git* (*http://git-scm.com/book*), and the full-size *Version Control with Git* by Jon Loeliger (O'Reilly). In addition, the Git software documentation ("man pages" on Unix) is generally well written and complete. So, why a *Git Pocket Guide*? The primary goal of this book is to provide a compact, readable introduction to Git for the new user, as well as a reference to common commands and procedures that will continue to be useful once you've already gotten some Git under your belt. The man pages are extensive and very detailed; sometimes, it's difficult to peruse them for just the information you need for simple operations, and you may need to refer to several different sections to pull together the pieces you need. The two books mentioned are similarly weighty tomes with a wealth of detail. This Pocket Guide is task oriented, organized around the basic functions you need from version control: making commits, fixing mistakes, merging, searching history, and so on. It also contains a streamlined technical introduction whose aim is to make sense of Git generally and facilitate understanding of the operations discussed, rather than completeness or depth for its own sake. The intent is to help you become productive with Git quickly and easily.

Since this book does not aim to be a complete reference to all of Git's capabilities, there are Git commands and functions that we do not discuss. We often mention these omissions explicitly, but some are tacit. Several more advanced features are just mentioned and described briefly so that you're aware of their existence, with a pointer to the relevant documentation. Also, the sections that cover specific commands usually do not list every possible option or mode of operation, but rather the most common or useful ones that fit into the discussion at hand. The goal is simplicity and economy of explanation, rather than exhaustive detail. We do provide frequent references to various portions of the Git documentation, where you can find more complete information on the current topic. This book should be taken as an introduction, an aid to understanding, and a complement to the full documentation, rather than as a replacement for it.

At the time of this writing in early 2013, Git is undergoing rapid development; new versions appear regularly with new features and changes to existing ones, so expect that by the time you read this, some alterations will already have occurred; that's just the nature of technical writing. This book describes Git as of version 1.8.2.

Conventions Used in This Book

Here are a few general remarks and conventions to keep in mind while reading this book.

Unix

Git was created in the Unix environment, originally in fact both for and by people working on the core of the Linux operating system. Though it has been ported to other platforms, it is still most popular on Unix variants, and its commands, design, and terminology all strongly reflect its origin. Especially in a Pocket Guide format, it would be distracting to have constant asides on minor differences with other platforms, so for simplicity and uniformity, this book assumes Unix generally in its descriptions and choice of examples.

Shell

All command-line examples are given using the *bash* shell syntax. Git uses characters that are special to *bash* and other shells as well, such as *, ~, and ?. Remember that you will need to quote these in order to prevent the shell from expanding them before Git sees them. For example, to see a log of changes pertaining to all C source files, you need something like this:

```
$ git log -- '*.c'
```

and not this:

```
$ git log -- *.c
```

The latter is unpredictable, as the shell will try to expand *.c in the current context. It might do any number of things; few of them are likely to be what you want.

The examples given in the book use such quoting as necessary.

Command Syntax

We employ common Unix conventions for indicating the syntax of commands, including:

- --{foo,bar} indicates the options --foo and --bar.

- Square brackets indicate an optional element that may appear or not; e.g., --where[=*location*] means that you may either use --where by itself (with some default location) or give a specific location, perhaps --where=Boston.

Typography

The following typographical conventions are used in this book:

Italic

    Indicates new terms; also, Git branches are normally given in italic, as opposed to other names such as tags and commit IDs, which are given in constant width. Titles to Unix man pages are also given in italics.

Constant width

> Used for program listings, as well as within paragraphs to refer to program elements such as variable or function names, databases, data types, environment variables, statements, and keywords.

Constant width bold

> Shows commands or other text that should be typed literally by the user.

Constant width italic

> Shows text that should be replaced with user-supplied values or by values determined by context.

TIP

These lines signify a tip, warning, caution, or general note.

Using Code Examples

This book is here to help you get your job done. In general, if this book includes code examples, you may use the code in this book in your programs and documentation. You do not need to contact us for permission unless you're reproducing a significant portion of the code. For example, writing a program that uses several chunks of code from this book does not require permission. Selling or distributing a CD-ROM of examples from O'Reilly books does require permission. Answering a question by citing this book and quoting example code does not require permission. Incorporating a significant amount of example code from this book into your product's documentation does require permission.

We appreciate, but do not require, attribution. An attribution usually includes the title, author, publisher, and ISBN. For example: "*Git Pocket Guide* by Richard E. Silverman (O'Reilly). Copyright 2013 Richard Silverman, 978-1-449-32586-2."

If you feel your use of code examples falls outside fair use or the permission given above, feel free to contact us at *permis sions@oreilly.com*.

Safari® Books Online

Safari Books Online is an on-demand digital library that delivers expert content in both book and video form from the world's leading authors in technology and business.

Technology professionals, software developers, web designers, and business and creative professionals use Safari Books Online as their primary resource for research, problem solving, learning, and certification training.

Safari Books Online offers a range of product mixes and pricing programs for organizations, government agencies, and individuals. Subscribers have access to thousands of books, training videos, and prepublication manuscripts in one fully searchable database from publishers like O'Reilly Media, Prentice Hall Professional, Addison-Wesley Professional, Microsoft Press, Sams, Que, Peachpit Press, Focal Press, Cisco Press, John Wiley & Sons, Syngress, Morgan Kaufmann, IBM Redbooks, Packt, Adobe Press, FT Press, Apress, Manning, New Riders, McGraw-Hill, Jones & Bartlett, Course Technology, and dozens more. For more information about Safari Books Online, please visit us online.

How to Contact Us

Please address comments and questions concerning this book to the publisher:

O'Reilly Media, Inc.
1005 Gravenstein Highway North
Sebastopol, CA 95472
800-998-9938 (in the United States or Canada)
707-829-0515 (international or local)
707-829-0104 (fax)

We have a web page for this book, where we list errata, examples, and any additional information. You can access this page at *http://oreil.ly/git_pocket_guide*.

To comment or ask technical questions about this book, send email to *bookquestions@oreilly.com*.

For more information about our books, courses, conferences, and news, see our website at *http://www.oreilly.com*.

Find us on Facebook: *http://facebook.com/oreilly*

Follow us on Twitter: *http://twitter.com/oreillymedia*

Watch us on YouTube: *http://www.youtube.com/oreillymedia*

Acknowledgments

I gratefully acknowledge the support and patience of everyone at O'Reilly involved in creating this book, especially my editors Meghan Blanchette and Mike Loukides, during a book-writing process with a few unexpected challenges along the way. I would also like to thank my technical reviewers: Robert G. Byrnes, Max Caceres, Robert P. J. Day, Bart Massey, and Lukas Toth. Their attention to detail and thoughtful criticism have made this a much better book than it would otherwise have been. All errors that survived their combined assault are mine and mine alone.

I dedicate this book to the memory of my grandmother, Eleanor Gorsuch Jefferies (19 May 1920–18 March 2012).

Richard E. Silverman
New York City, 15 April 2013

## CHAPTER 1

Understanding Git

In this initial chapter, we discuss how Git operates, defining important terms and concepts you should understand in order to use Git effectively.

Some tools and technologies lend themselves to a "black-box" approach, in which new users don't pay too much attention to how a tool works under the hood. You concentrate first on learning to manipulate the tool; the "why" and "how" can come later. Git's particular design, however, is better served by the opposite approach, in that a number of fundamental internal design decisions are reflected directly in how you use it. By understanding up front and in reasonable detail several key points about its operation, you will be able to come up to speed with Git more quickly and confidently, and be better prepared to continue learning on your own.

Thus, I encourage you to take the time to read this chapter first, rather than just jump over it to the more tutorial, hands-on chapters that follow (most of which assume a basic grasp of the material presented here, in any case). You will probably find that your understanding and command of Git will grow more easily if you do.

Overview

We start by introducing some basic terms and ideas, the general notion of branching, and the usual mechanism by which you share your work with others in Git.

Terminology

A Git project is represented by a "repository," which contains the complete history of the project from its inception. A repository in turn consists of a set of individual snapshots of project content—collections of files and directories—called "commits." A single commit comprises the following:

A project content snapshot, called a "tree"
> A structure of nested files and directories representing a complete state of the project

The "author" identification
> Name, email address, and date/time (or "timestamp") indicating who made the changes that resulted in this project state and when

The "committer" identification
> The same information about the person who added this commit to the repository (which may be different from the author)

A "commit message"
> Text used to comment on the changes made by this commit

A list of zero or more "parent commits"
> References to other commits in the same repository, indicating immediately preceding states of the project content

The set of all commits in a repository, connected by lines indicating their parent commits, forms a picture called the repository "commit graph," shown in Figure 1-1.

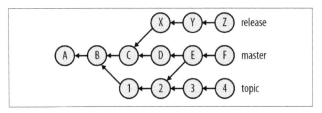

Figure 1-1. The repository "commit graph"

The letters and numbers here represent commits, and arrows point from a commit to its parents. Commit A has no parents and is called a "root commit"; it was the initial commit in this repository's history. Most commits have a single parent, indicating that they evolved in a straightforward way from a single previous state of the project, usually incorporating a set of related changes made by one person. Some commits, here just the one labeled E, have multiple parents and are called "merge commits." This indicates that the commit reconciles the changes made on distinct branches of the commit graph, often combining contributions made separately by different people.

Since it is normally clear from context in which direction the history proceeds—usually, as here, parent commits appear to the left of their children—we will omit the arrow heads in such diagrams from now on.

Branches

The labels on the right side of this picture—*master*, *topic*, and *release*—denote "branches." The branch name refers to the latest commit on that branch; here, commits F, 4, and Z, respectively, are called the "tip" of the branch. The branch itself is defined as the collection of all commits in the graph that are reachable from the tip by following the parent arrows backward along the history. Here, the branches are:

- *release* = {A, B, C, X, Y, Z}
- *master* = {A, B, C, D, E, F, 1, 2}

- *topic* = {A, B, 1, 2, 3, 4}

Note that branches can overlap; here, commits 1 and 2 are on both the *master* and *topic* branches, and commits A and B are on all three branches. Usually, you are "on" a branch, looking at the content corresponding to the tip commit on that branch. When you change some files and add a new commit containing the changes (called "committing to the repository"), the branch name advances to the new commit, which in turn points to the old commit as its sole parent; this is the way branches move forward. From time to time, you will tell Git to "merge" several branches (most often two, but there can be more), tying them together as at commit E in Figure 1-1. The same branches can be merged repeatedly over time, showing that they continued to progress separately while you periodically combined their contents.

The first branch in a new repository is named *master* by default, and it's customary to use that name if there is only one branch in the repository, or for the branch that contains the main line of development (if that makes sense for your project). You are not required to do so, however, and there is nothing special about the name "master" apart from convention, and its use as a default by some commands.

Sharing Work

There are two contexts in which version control is useful: private and public. When working on your own, it's useful to commit "early and often," so that you can explore different ideas and make changes freely without worrying about recovering earlier work. Such commits are likely to be somewhat disorganized and have cryptic commit messages, which is fine because they need to be intelligible only to you, and for a short period of time. Once a portion of your work is finished and you're ready to share it with others, though, you may want to reorganize those commits, to make them well-factored with regard to reusability of the changes being made (especially with software), and to give them meaningful, well-written commit messages.

In centralized version control systems, the acts of committing a change and publishing it for others to see are one and the same: the unit of publication is the commit, and committing requires publishing (applying the change to the central repository where others can immediately see it). This makes it difficult to use version control in both private and public contexts. By separating committing and publishing, and giving you tools with which to edit and reorganize existing commits, Git encourages better use of version control overall.

With Git, sharing work between repositories happens via operations called "push" and "pull": you pull changes from a remote repository and push changes to it. To work on a project, you "clone" it from an existing repository, possibly over a network via protocols such as HTTP and SSH. Your clone is a full copy of the original, including all project history, completely functional on its own. In particular, you do not need to contact the first repository again in order to examine the history of your clone or commit to it—however, your new repository does retain a reference to the original one, called a "remote." This reference includes the state of the branches in the remote as of the last time you pulled from it; these are called "remote tracking" branches. If the original repository contains two branches named *master* and *topic*, their remote-tracking branches in your clone appear qualified with the name of the remote (by default called "origin"): *origin/master* and *origin/topic*.

Most often, the *master* branch will be automatically checked out for you when you first clone the repository; Git initially checks out whatever the current branch is in the remote repository. If you later ask to check out the *topic* branch, Git sees that there isn't yet a local branch with that name—but since there is a remote-tracking branch named *origin/topic*, it automatically creates a branch named *topic* and sets *origin/topic* as its "upstream" branch. This relationship causes the push/pull mechanism to keep the changes made to these branches in sync as they evolve in both your repository and in the remote.

When you pull, Git updates the remote-tracking branches with the current state of the origin repository; conversely, when you push, it updates the remote with any changes you've made to corresponding local branches. If these changes conflict, Git prompts you to merge the changes before accepting or sending them, so that neither side loses any history in the process.

If you're familiar with CVS or Subversion, a useful conceptual shift is to consider that a "commit" in those systems is analogous to a Git "push." You still commit in Git, of course, but that affects only your repository and is not visible to anyone else until you push those commits—and you are free to edit, reorganize, or delete your commits until you do so.

The Object Store

Now, we discuss the ideas just introduced in more detail, starting with the heart of a Git repository: its *object store*. This is a database that holds just four kinds of items: *blobs*, *trees*, *commits*, and *tags*.

Blob

A *blob* is an opaque chunk of data, a string of bytes with no further internal structure as far as Git is concerned. The content of a file under version control is represented as a blob. This does not mean the implementation of blobs is naive; Git uses sophisticated compression and transmission techniques to handle blobs efficiently.

Every version of a file in Git is represented as a whole, with its own blob containing the file's complete contents. This stands in contrast to some other systems, in which file versions are represented as a series of differences from one revision to the next, starting with a base version. Various trade-offs stem from this design point. One is that Git may use more storage space; on the other hand, it does not have to reconstruct files to retrieve them by applying layers of differences, so it can be faster. This design increases reliability by increasing redundancy: corruption of one blob affects only that file version, whereas corruption of a difference affects all versions coming after that one.

Tree

A Git *tree*, by itself, is actually what one might usually think of as one level of a tree: it represents a single level of directory structure in the repository content. It contains a list of items, each of which has:

- A filename and associated information that Git tracks, such as its Unix permissions ("mode bits") and file type; Git can handle Unix "symbolic links" as well as regular files.

- A pointer to another object. If that object is a blob, then this item represents a file; if it's another tree, a directory.

There is an ambiguity here: when we say "tree," do we mean a single object as just described, or the collection of all such objects reachable from it by following the pointers recursively until we reach the terminal blobs—that is, a "tree" in the more usual sense? It is the latter notion of tree that this data structure is used to represent, of course, and fortunately, it is seldom necessary in practice to make the distinction. When we say "tree," we will normally mean the entire hierarchy of tree and blob objects; when necessary, we will use the phrase "tree object" to refer to the specific, individual data structure component.

A Git tree, then, represents a portion of the repository content at one point in time: a snapshot of a particular directory's content, including that of all directories beneath it.

Commit

A version control system manages content changes, and the *commit* is the fundamental unit of change in Git. A commit is a snapshot of the entire repository content, together with identifying information, and the relationship of this historical repository state to other recorded states as the content has evolved over time. Specifically, a commit consists of:

- A pointer to a tree containing the complete state of the repository content at one point in time.

- Ancillary information about this change: who was responsible for the content (the "author"); who introduced the change into the repository (the "committer"); and the time and date for both those things. The act of adding a commit object to the repository is called "making a commit," or "committing (to the repository)."

- A list of zero or more other commit objects, called the "parents" of this commit. The parent relationship has no intrinsic meaning; however, the normal ways of making a commit are meant to indicate that the commit's repository state was derived by the author from those of its parents in some meaningful way (e.g., by adding a feature or fixing a bug). A chain of commits, each having a single parent, indicates a simple evolution of repository state by discrete steps (and as we'll see, this constitutes a branch). When a commit has more than one parent, this indicates a "merge," in which the committer has incorporated the changes from multiple lines of development into a single commit. We'll define branches and merges more precisely in a moment.

Of course, at least one commit in the repository must have zero parents, or else the repository would either be infinitely large or have loops in the commit graph, which is not allowed (see the description of a "DAG" next). This is called a "root commit," and most often, there is only one root commit in a repository—the initial one created when the repository was started. However, you can introduce multiple root commits if you want; the command `git checkout --orphan` does this. This incorporates multiple independent histories into a repository, perhaps in order to collect the contents of previously separate projects (see "Importing Disconnected History" on page 154).

Author versus Committer

The separate author and committer information—name, email address, and timestamp—reflect the creation of the commit content and its addition to the repository, respectively. These are initially the same, but may later become distinct with the use of certain Git commands. For example, `git cherry-pick` replicates an existing commit by reapplying the changes introduced by that commit in another context. Cherry-picking carries forward the author information from the original commit, while adding new committer information. This preserves the identification and origin date of the changes, while indicating that they were applied at another point in the repository at a later date, possibly by a different person. A bugfix cherry-picked from one repository to another might look like this:

```
$ git log --format=fuller
commit d404534d
Author:     Eustace Maushaven <eustace@qoxp.net>
AuthorDate: Thu Nov 29 01:58:13 2012 -0500
```

```
Commit:     Richard E. Silverman <res@mlitg.com>
CommitDate: Tue Feb 26 17:01:33 2013 -0500

    Fix spin-loop bug in k5_sendto_kdc

    In the second part of the first pass over the
    server list, we passed the wrong list pointer to
    service_fds, causing it to see only a subset of
    the server entries corresponding to sel_state.
    This could cause service_fds to spin if an event
    is reported on an fd not in the subset.

    ---
    cherry-picked from upstream by res
    upstream commit 2b06a22f7fd8ec01fb27a7335125290b8…
```

Other operations that do this are git rebase and git filter-branch; like git cherry-pick, they too create new commits based on existing ones.

Cryptographic Signature

A commit may also be signed using GnuPG, with:

```
$ git commit --gpg-sign[=keyid]
```

See "Cryptographic Keys" on page 37 regarding Git's selection of a key identifier.

A cryptographic signature binds the commit to a particular real-world personal identity attached to the key used for signing; it verifies that the commit's contents are the same now as they were when that person signed it. The *meaning* of the signature, though, is a matter of interpretation. If I sign a commit, it might mean that I glanced at the diff; verified that the software builds; ran a test suite; prayed to Cthulhu for a bug-free release; or did none of these. Aside from being a convention among the users of the repository, I can also put the intention of my signature in the commit message; presumably, I will not sign a commit without at least reading its message.

Tag

A *tag* serves to distinguish a particular commit by giving it a human-readable name in a namespace reserved for this purpose. Otherwise, commits are in a sense anonymous, normally referred to only by their position along some branch, which changes with time as the branch evolves (and may even disappear if the branch is later deleted). The tag content consists of the name of the person making the tag, a timestamp, a reference to the commit being tagged, and free-form text similar to a commit message.

A tag can have any meaning you like; often, it identifies a particular software release, with a name like `coolutil-1.0-rc2` and a suitable message. You can cryptographically sign a tag just as you can a commit, in order to verify the tag's authenticity.

NOTE

There are actually two kinds of tags in Git: "lightweight" and "annotated." This section refers to annotated tags, which are represented as a separate kind of object in the repository database. A lightweight tag is entirely different; it is simply a name pointing directly to a commit (see the upcoming section on refs to understand how such names work generally).

Object IDs and SHA-1

A fundamental design element of Git is that the object store uses *content-based addressing.* Some other systems assign identifiers to their equivalent of commits that are relative to one another in some way, and reflect the order in which commits were made. For example, file revisions in CVS are dotted strings of numbers such as 2.17.1.3, in which (usually) the numbers are simply counters: they increment as you make changes or add branches. This means that there is no instrinsic relationship between a revision and its identifier; revision 2.17.1.3 in someone else's CVS repository, if it exists, will almost certainly be different from yours.

Git, on the other hand, assigns object identifiers based on an object's contents, rather than on its relationship to other objects, using a mathematical technique called a *hash function*. A hash function takes an arbitrary block of data and produces a sort of fingerprint for it. The particular hash function Git uses, called SHA-1, produces a 160-bit fixed-length value for any data object you feed it, no matter how large.

The usefulness of hash-based object identifiers in Git depends on treating the SHA-1 hash of an object as unique; we assume that if two objects have the same SHA-1 fingerprint, then they are in fact *the same object.* From this property flow a number of key points:

Single-instance store

Git never stores more than one copy of a file. It can't—if you add a second copy of the file, it will hash the file contents to find its SHA-1 object ID, look in the database, and find that it's already there. This is also a consequence of the separation of a file's contents from its name. Trees map filenames onto blobs in a separate step, to determine the contents of a particular filename at any given commit, but Git does not consider the name or other properties of a file when storing it, only its contents.

Efficient comparisons

As part of managing change, Git is constantly comparing things: files against other files, changed files against existing commits, as well as one commit against another. It compares whole repository states, which might encompass hundreds or thousands of files, but it does so with great efficiency because of hashing. When comparing two trees, for example, if it finds that two subtrees have the same ID, it can immediately stop comparing those portions of the trees, no matter how many layers of directories and files might remain. Why? We said earlier that a tree object contains "pointers" to its child objects, either blobs or other trees. Well, those pointers are the objects' SHA-1 IDs. If two trees have the same ID, then they have the same contents, which means they must contain the same child object IDs, which means that in turn *those* objects must also be the same! Inductively, we see immediately that in fact, the entire contents of the two trees must be identical, if the uniqueness property assumed previously holds.

Database sharing

Git repositories can share their object databases at any level with impunity because there can be no aliasing; the binding between an ID and the content to which it refers is immutable. One repository cannot mess up another's object store by changing the data out from under it; in that sense, an object store can only be expanded, not changed. We do still have to worry about *removing* objects that another database is using, but that's a much easier problem to solve.

Much of the power of Git stems from content-based addressing —but if you think for a moment, it's based on a lie! We are claiming that the SHA-1 hash of a data object is unique, but that's mathematically impossible: because the hash function output has a fixed length of 160 bits, there are exactly 2^{160} IDs—but infinitely many potential data objects to hash. There *have* to be duplications, called "hash collisions." The whole system appears fatally flawed.

The solution to this problem lies in what constitutes a "good" hash function, and the odd-sounding notion that while SHA-1 cannot be mathematically collision-free, it is what we might call *effectively* so. For the practical purposes of Git, I'm not necessarily concerned if there are in fact other files that might have the same ID as one of mine; what really matters is whether any of those files are at all likely to ever appear in my project, or in anyone else's. Maybe all the other files are over 10 trillion bytes long, or will never match any program or text in any programming, object, or natural language ever invented by humanity. This is exactly a property (among others) that researchers endeavor to build into hash functions: the relationship between changes in the input and output is extremely sensitive and wildly unpredictable. Changing a single bit in a file causes its SHA-1 hash to change radically, and flipping a different bit in that file, or the same bit in a different file, will scramble the hash in a way that has no recognizable relationship to the other changes. Thus, it is not that SHA-1 hash collisions cannot happen—it is just that we believe them to be so astronomically unlikely in practice that we simply don't care.

Of course, discussing precise mathematical topics in general terms is fraught with hazard; this description is intended to communicate the essence of why we rely upon SHA-1 to do its job, not to prove anything rigorously or even to give justification for these claims.

Security

SHA-1 stands for "Secure Hash Algorithm 1," and its name reflects the fact that it was designed for use in cryptography. "Hashing" is a basic technique in computer science, with applications to many areas besides security, including signal processing, searching and sorting algorithms, and networking hardware. A "cryptographically secure" hash function like SHA-1 has related but distinct properties to those already mentioned with respect to Git; it is not just extraordinarily unlikely that two distinct trees arising in practice will produce the same commit ID, but it should also be effectively impossible for someone to deliberately find two such trees, or to find a second tree with the same ID as a given one. These features make a hash function useful in security as well as for more general purposes, since with them it can defend against deliberate tampering as well as ordinary or accidental changes to data.

Because SHA-1 is a cryptographic hash function, Git inherits certain security properties from its use of SHA-1 as well as operational ones. If I tag a particular commit of security-sensitive software, it is not feasible for an attacker to substitute a commit with the same ID in which he has embedded a backdoor; as long as I record the commit ID securely and compare it correctly, the repository is tamper proof in this regard. As explained earlier, the chained use of SHA-1 causes the tag's ID to cover the entire content of the tagged commit's tree. The addition of GnuPG digital signatures allows individuals to vouch for the contents of entire repository states and history, in a way that is impractical to forge.

Cryptographic research is always ongoing, though, and computing power increases every year; other hash functions such as MD5 that were once considered secure have been deprecated due to such advances. We have developed more secure versions of SHA itself, in fact, and as of this writing in early 2013, serious weaknesses in SHA-1 have recently been discovered. The criteria used to appraise hash functions for cryptographic use are very conservative, so these weaknesses are more theoretical than practical at the moment, but they are meaningful nonetheless. The good news is that further cryptographic breaks of SHA-1 will not affect the usefulness of Git as a version control system per se; that is, make it more likely in practice that Git will treat distinct commits as identical (that would be disastrous). They *will* affect the security properties Git enjoys as a result of using SHA-1, but those, while important, are critical to a smaller number of people (and those security goals can mostly be met in other ways if need be). In any case, it will be possible to switch Git to using a different hash function when it becomes necessary—and given the current state of research, it would probably be wise to do that sooner rather than later.

Where Objects Live

In a Git repository, objects are stored under *.git/objects*. They may be stored individually as "loose" objects, one per file with pathnames built from their object IDs:

```
$ find .git/objects -type f
.git/objects/08/5cf6be546e0b950e0cf7c530bdc78a6d5a78db
.git/objects/0d/55bed3a35cf47eefff69beadce1213b1f64c39
.git/objects/19/38cbe70ea103d7185a3831fd1f12db8c3ae2d3
.git/objects/1a/473cac853e6fc917724dfc6cbdf5a7479c1728
.git/objects/20/5f6b799e7d5c2524468ca006a0131aa57ecce7
...
```

They may also be collected into more compact data structures called "packs," which appear as paired *.idx* and *.pack* files:

```
$ ls .git/objects/pack/
pack-a18ec63201e3a5ac58704460b0dc7b30e4c05418.idx
pack-a18ec63201e3a5ac58704460b0dc7b30e4c05418.pack
```

Git automatically rearranges the object store over time to improve performance; for example, when it sees that there are many loose objects, it automatically coalesces them into packs (though you can do this by hand; see *git-repack(1)*). Don't assume that objects will be represented in any particular way; always use Git commands to access the object database, rather than digging around in *.git* yourself.

The Commit Graph

The collection of all commits in a repository forms what in mathematics is called a *graph*: visually, a set of objects with lines drawn between some pairs of them. In Git, the lines represent the commit parent relationship previously explained, and this structure is called the "commit graph" of the repository.

Because of the way Git works, there is some extra structure to this graph: the lines can be drawn with arrows pointing in one direction because a commit refers to its parent, but not the other way around (we'll see later the necessity and significance of this). Again using a mathematical term, this makes the graph "directed." The commit graph might be a simple linear history, as shown in Figure 1-2.

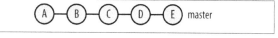

Figure 1-2. A linear commit graph

Or a complex picture involving many branches and merges, as shown in Figure 1-3.

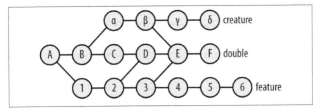

Figure 1-3. A more complex commit graph

Those are the next topics we'll touch on.

What's a DAG?

Git, by design, will not ever produce a graph that contains a loop; that is, a way to follow the arrows from one commit to another so that you arrive at the same commit twice (think what that could possibly mean in terms of a history of changes!). This is called being "acyclic": not having a cycle, or loop. Thus the commit graph is technically a "directed acyclic graph," or DAG for short.

Refs

Git defines two kinds of references, or named pointers, which it calls "refs":

- A simple ref, which points directly to an object ID (usually a commit or tag)

- A *symbolic ref* (or *symref*), which points to another ref (either simple or symbolic)

These are analogous to "hard links" and "symbolic links" in a Unix filesystem.

Git uses refs to name things, including commits, branches, and tags. Refs inhabit a hierarchical namespace separated by slashes (as with Unix filenames), starting at refs/. A new repository has at least `refs/tags/` and `refs/heads/`, to hold the names of tags and local branches, respectively. There is also `refs/remotes/`, holding names referring to other repositories; these contain beneath them the ref namespaces of those repositories, and are used in push and pull operations. For example, when you clone a repository, Git creates a "remote" named `origin` referring to the source repository.

There are various defaults, which means that you don't often have to refer to a ref by its full name; for example, in branch operations, Git implicitly looks in `refs/heads/` for the name you give.

Related Commands

These are low-level commands that directly display, change, or delete refs. You don't ordinarily need these, as Git usually handles refs automatically as part of dealing with the objects they represent, such as branches and tags. If you change refs directly, be sure you know what you're doing!

git `show-ref`
    Display refs and the objects to which they refer

git `symbolic-ref`
    Deals with symbolic refs specifically

git `update-ref`
    Change the value of a ref

git `for-each-ref`
    Apply an action to a set of refs

Branches

A Git branch is the simplest thing possible: a pointer to a commit, as a ref. Or rather, that is its implementation; the branch itself is defined as all points reachable in the commit graph from the named commit (the "tip" of the branch). The special ref HEAD determines what branch you are on; if HEAD is a symbolic ref for an existing branch, then you are "on" that branch. If, on the other hand, HEAD is a simple ref directly naming a commit by its SHA-1 ID, then you are not "on" any branch, but rather in "detached HEAD" mode, which happens when you check out some earlier commit to examine. Let's see:

```
# HEAD points to the master branch
$ git symbolic-ref HEAD
refs/heads/master

# Git agrees; I'm on the master branch.
$ git branch
* master

# Check out a tagged commit, not at a branch tip.
$ git checkout mytag
Note: checking out 'mytag'.

You are in 'detached HEAD' state...

# Confirmed: HEAD is no longer a symbolic ref.
$ git symbolic-ref HEAD
fatal: ref HEAD is not a symbolic ref
```

```
# What is it? A commit ID...
$ git rev-parse HEAD
1c7ed724236402d7426606b03ee38f34c662be27

# ... which matches the commit referred to by the
# tag.
$ git rev-parse mytag^{commit}
1c7ed724236402d7426606b03ee38f34c662be27

# Git agrees; we're not on any branch.
$ git branch
* (no branch)
  master
```

The HEAD commit is also often referred to as the "current" commit. If you are on a branch, it may also be called the "last" or "tip" commit of the branch.

A branch evolves over time; thus, if you are on the branch *master* and make a commit, Git does the following:

1. Creates a new commit with your changes to the repository content

2. Makes the commit at the current tip of the *master* branch the parent of the new commit

3. Adds the new commit to the object store

4. Changes the *master* branch (specifically, the ref refs/heads/master) to point to the new commit

In other words, Git adds the new commit to the end of the branch using the commit's parent pointer, and advances the branch ref to the new commit.

Note a few consequences of this model:

- Considered individually, a commit is not intrinsically a part of any branch. There is nothing in the commit itself to tell you by name which branches it is or may once have been on; branch membership is a consequence of the commit graph and the current branch pointers.

- "Deleting" a branch means simply deleting the corresponding ref; it has no immediate effect on the object store. In particular, deleting a branch does not delete any commits. What it may do, however, is make certain commits *uninteresting,* in that they are no longer on any branch (that is, no longer reachable in the commit graph from any branch tip or tag). If this state persists, Git will eventually remove such commits from the object store as part of garbage collection. Until that happens, though, if you have an abandoned commit's ID you can still directly access it perfectly well by its SHA-1 name; the Git *reflog* (`git log -g`) is useful in this regard.

- By this definition, a branch can include more than just commits made while on that branch; it also contains commits from branches that flow into this one via an earlier merge. For example: here, the branch *topic* was merged into *master* at commit C, then both branches continued to evolve separately, as shown in Figure 1-4.

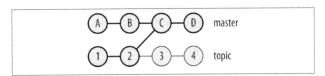

Figure 1-4. A simple merge

At this point, `git log` on the *master* branch shows not only commits A through D as you would expect, but also commits 1 and 2, since they are also reachable from D via C. This may be surprising, but it's just a different way of defining the idea of a branch: as the set of all commits that contributed content to the latest commit. You can generally get the effect of looking "only at the history of this branch"—even though that's not really well defined —with `git log --first-parent`.

The Index

The Git "index" often seems a bit mysterious to people: some invisible, ineffable place where changes are "staged" until they're committed. The talk about "staging changes" in the index also suggests that it holds only changes, as if it were a collection of diffs waiting to be applied. The truth is different and quite simple, and critical to grasp in order to understand Git well. The index is an independent data structure, separate from both your working tree and from any commit. It is simply a list of file pathnames together with associated attributes, usually including the ID of a blob in the object database holding the data for a version of that file. You can see the current contents of the index with `git ls-files`:

```
$ git ls-files --abbrev --stage
100644 2830ea0b 0       TODO
100644 a4d2acee 0       VERSION
100644 ce30ff91 0       acinclude.m4
100644 236d5f93 0       configure.ac
...
```

The `--stage` option means to show just the index; `git ls-files` can show various combinations and subsets of the index and your working tree, generally. If you were to delete or change any of the listed files in your working tree, this would not affect the output of this command at all; it's not looking at them. Key facts about the index:

- The index is the implicit source of the content for a normal commit. When you use `git commit` (without supplying specific pathnames), you might think that it creates the new commit based on your working files. It does not; instead, it simply realizes the current index as a new tree object, and makes the new commit from that. This is why you need to "stage" a changed file in the index with `git add` in order for it to be part of the next commit.

- The index does not just contain changes to be made on the next commit; it *is* the next commit, a complete catalog of the files that will be included in the tree of the next commit (recall that each commit refers to a tree object that is a complete snapshot of the repository content). When you check out a branch, Git resets the index to match the tip commit of that branch; you then modify the index with commands such as `git add/mv/rm` to indicate changes to be part of the next commit.

- `git add` does not just note in the index that a file has changed; it actually adds the current file content to the object database as a new blob, and updates the index entry for that file to refer to that blob. This is why `git commit` is always fast, even if you're making lots of changes: all the actual data has already been stored by preceding `git add` commands.

  An implication of this behavior that occasionally confuses people is that if you change a file, `git add` it, then change it again, it is the version you last added to the index, *not* the one in your working tree, that is part of the next commit. `git status` shows this explicitly, by listing the same file as having both "changes to be committed" and "changes not staged for commit."

- Similar to `git commit`, `git diff` without arguments also has the index as an implicit operand; it shows the differences between your working tree and the *index*, rather than the current commit. Initially these are the same, as the index matches the last commit after a clean checkout or commit. As you make changes to your working files, these show up in the output of `git diff`, then disappear as you add the corresponding files. The idea is that `git diff` shows changes not yet staged for commit, so you can see what you have yet to deal with (or have deliberately not included) as you prepare the next commit. `git diff --staged` shows the opposite: the differences between the index and the current commit (that is, the changes that are about to be committed).

Merging

Merging is the complement of branching in version control: a branch allows you to work simultaneously with others on a particular set of files, whereas a merge allows you to later combine separate work on two or more branches that diverged earlier from a common ancestor commit. Here are two common merge scenarios:

1. You are working by yourself on a software project. You decide to explore refactoring your code in a certain way, so you make a branch named *refactor* off of the *master* branch. You can make any changes you like on the *refactor* branch without disturbing the main line of development.

   After a while, you're happy with the refactoring you've done and want to keep it, so you switch to the *master* branch and run `git merge refactor`. Git applies the changes you've made on both branches since they diverged, asking for your help in resolving any conflicts, then commits the result. You delete the *refactor* branch, and move on.

2. You have been working on the *master* branch of a cloned repository and have made several commits over a day or two. You then run `git pull` to update your clone with the latest work committed to the origin repository. It happens that others have also committed to the origin *master* branch in the meantime, so Git performs an automatic merge of *master* and *origin/master* and commits this to your *master* branch. You can then continue with your work or push to the origin repository now that you have incorporated its latest changes with your own. See "Push and Pull" on page 26.

There are two aspects to merging in Git: content and history.

Merging Content

What it means to successfully "merge" two or more sets of
changes to the same file depends on the nature of the contents.
Git will try to merge automatically, and often call it a success if
the two changesets altered non-overlapping portions of the file.
Whether *you* will call that a success, however, is a different question. If the file is chapter three of your next novel, then perhaps
such a merge would be fine if you were making minor grammar
and style corrections. If you were reworking the plot line, on the
other hand, the results could be less useful—perhaps you added
a paragraph on one branch that depends on details contained in
a later paragraph that was deleted on another branch. Even if the
contents are programming source code, such a merge is not
guaranteed to be useful. You could change two separate subrou-
tines in a way that causes them to fail when actually used; they
might now make incompatible assumptions about some shared
data structure, for example. Git doesn't even check to see that
your code still compiles; that's up to you.

Within these limitations, though, Git has very sophisticated
mechanisms for presenting merge conflicts and helping you to
resolve them. It is optimized for the most common use case:
line-oriented textual data, often in computer programming languages. It has different strategies and options for determining
"matching" portions of files, which you can use when the defaults
don't produce adequate results. You can interactively choose sets
of changes to apply, skip, or further edit. To handle complex
merges, Git works smoothly with external merge tools such as
araxis, *emerge*, and *kdiff*, or with custom merge tools you write
yourself.

Merging History

When Git has done what it can automatically, and you have resolved any remaining conflicts, it's time to commit the result. If
we just make a commit to the current branch as usual, though,
we've lost critical information: the fact that a merge occurred at
all, and which branches were involved. You might remember to

include this information in the commit message, but it's best not to depend on that; more importantly, Git needs to know about the merge in order to do a good job of merging in the future. Otherwise, the next time you merge the same branches (say, to periodically update one with continuing changes on the other), Git won't know which changes have already been merged and which are new. It may end up flagging as conflicts changes you have already considered and handled, or automatically applying changes you previously decided to discard.

The way Git records the fact of a merge is very simple. Recall from "The Object Store" on page 6 that a commit has a list of zero or more "parent commits." The initial commit in a repository has no parents, and a simple commit to a branch has just one. When you commit as part of a merge, Git lists the tip commits of all branches involved in the merge as the parents of the new commit. This is in fact the definition of a "merge commit": a commit having more than one parent. This information, recorded as part of the commit graph, allows visualization tools to detect and display merges in a helpful and unambiguous way. It also lets Git find an appropriate base version for comparison in later merging of the same or related branches when they have diverged again, avoiding the duplication mentioned earlier; this is called the "merge base."

Push and Pull

You use the commands `git pull` and `git push` to update the state of one repository from that of another. Usually, one of these repositories was cloned from the other; in this context, `git pull` updates my clone with recent work added to the original repository, whereas `git push` contributes my work in the other direction.

There is sometimes confusion over the relationship between a repository and the one from which it was cloned. We're told that all repositories are equal, yet there seems to be an asymmetry in the original/clone relationship. Pulling automatically updates this repository from the original, so how interconnected are they?

Will the clone still be usable if the original goes away? Are there branches in my repository that are somehow pointers to content in another repository? If so, that doesn't sound as if they're truly independent.

Fortunately, as with most things in Git, the situation is actually very simple; we just need to precisely define the terms at hand. The central thing to remember is that with regard to content, a repository consists of two things: an object store and a set of refs —that is, a commit graph and a set of branch names and tags that call out those commits that are of interest. When you clone a repository, such as with `git clone server:dir/repo`, here's what Git does:

1. Creates a new repository.

2. Adds a *remote* named "origin" to refer to the repository being cloned in *.git/config*:

   ```
   [remote "origin"]
       fetch = +refs/heads/*:refs/remotes/origin/*
       url = server:dir/repo
   ```

   The `fetch` value here, called a *refspec*, specifies a correspondence between sets of refs in the two repositories: the pattern on the left side of the colon names refs in the remote, and the spec indicates with the pattern on the right side where the corresponding refs should appear in the local repository. In this case, it means: "Keep copies of the branch refs of the remote `origin` in its local namespace in this repository, `refs/remotes/origin/`."

3. Runs `git fetch origin`, which updates our local refs for the remote's branches (creating them in this case), and asks the remote to send any objects we need to complete the history for those refs (in the case of this new repository, all of them).

4. Finally, Git checks out the remote's current branch (its HEAD ref), leaving you with a working tree to look at. You

can select a different initial branch to check out with
`--branch`, or suppress the checkout entirely with `-n`.

Suppose we know the other repository has two branches, *master* and *beta*. Having cloned it, we see:

```
$ git branch
* master
```

Very well, we're on the *master* branch, but where's the *beta* branch? It appears to be missing until we use the `--all` switch:

```
$ git branch --all
* master
  remotes/origin/HEAD -> origin/master
  remotes/origin/master
  remotes/origin/beta
```

Aha! There it is. This makes some sense: we have copies of the refs for both branches in the origin repository, just where the origin refspec says they should be, and there is also the HEAD ref from the origin, which told Git the default branch to check out. The curious thing now is: what is this duplicate master branch, outside of origin, that is the one we're actually on? And why did we have to give an extra option to see all these in the first place?

The answer lies in the purpose of the origin refs: they're called *remote-tracking* refs, and they are markers showing us the current state of those branches on the remote (as of the last time we checked in with the remote via fetch or pull). In adding to the *master* branch, you don't want to actually directly update your tracking branch with a commit of your own; then it would no longer reflect the remote repository state (and on your next pull, it would just discard your additions by resetting the tracking branch to match the remote). So, Git created a new branch with the same name in your local namespace, starting at the same commit as the remote branch:

```
$ git show-ref --abbrev master
d2e46a81 refs/heads/master
d2e46a81 refs/remotes/origin/master
```

The abbreviated SHA-1 values on the left are the commit IDs; note that they are the same, and recall that `refs/heads/` is the implicit namespace for local branches. Now, as you add to your *master* branch, it will diverge from the remote master, which reflects the actual state of affairs.

The final piece here is the behavior of your local *master* branch in regard to the remote. Your intention is presumably to share your work with others as an update to their *master* branches; also, you'd like to keep abreast of changes made to this branch in the remote while you're working. To that end, Git has added some configuration for this branch in *.git/config*:

```
[branch "master"]
        remote = origin
        merge = refs/heads/master
```

This means that when you use `git pull` while on this branch, Git will automatically attempt to merge in any changes made to the corresponding remote branch since the last pull. This configuration affects the behavior of other commands as well, including `fetch`, `push`, and `rebase`.

Finally, Git has a special convenience for `git checkout` if you try to check out a branch that doesn't exist, but a corresponding branch *does* exist as part of a remote. It will automatically set up a local branch by the same name with the upstream configuration just demonstrated. For example:

```
$ git checkout beta
Branch beta set up to track remote branch beta from
origin. Switched to a new branch 'beta'

$ git branch --all
* beta
  master
  remotes/origin/HEAD -> origin/master
  remotes/origin/beta
  remotes/origin/master
```

Having explained remote-tracking branches, we can now say succinctly what the `push` and `pull` operations do:

`git pull`

> Runs `git fetch` on the remote for the current branch, updating the remote's local tracking refs and obtaining any new objects needed to complete the history of those refs: that is, all commits, tags, trees, and blobs reachable from the new branch tips. Then it tries to update the current local branch to match the corresponding branch in the remote. If only one side has added content to the branch, then this will succeed, and is called a *fast-forward* update since one ref is simply moved forward along the branch to catch up with the other.
>
> If both sides have committed to the branch, however, then Git has to do something to incorporate both versions of the branch history into one shared version. By default, this is a merge: Git merges the remote branch into the local one, producing a new commit that refers to both sides of the history via its parent pointers. Another possibility is to *rebase* instead, which attempts to rewrite your divergent commits as new ones at the tip of the updated remote branch (see "Pull with Rebase" on page 89).

`git push`

> Attempts to update the corresponding branch in the remote with your local state, sending any objects the remote needs to complete the new history. This will fail if the update would be non–fast-forward as described earlier (i.e., would cause the remote to discard history), and Git will suggest that you first pull in order to resolve the discrepancies and produce an acceptable update.

Notes

1. It should be clear from this description that nothing about the remote-tracking branches ties the operation of your repository to the remote. Each is just a branch in your repository like any other branch, a ref pointing to a particular commit. They are only "remote" in their intention: they track the state of corresponding branches in the remote, and they are periodically updated via `git pull`.

2. It can be momentarily confusing if you clone a repository, use `git log` on a branch you know is in the remote, and it fails—because you don't have a *local* branch by that name (yet); it's only in the remote. You don't have to check it out and set up a local branch just to examine it, though; you can specify the remote-tracking branch by name: `git log origin/foo`.

3. A repository can have any number of remotes, set up at any time; see *git-remote(1)*. If the original repository you cloned from is no longer valid, you can fix the URL by editing *.git/config* or with `git remote set-url`, or remove it entirely with `git remote rm` (which will remove the corresponding remote-tracking branches as well).

## CHAPTER 2

Getting Started

In this chapter, you'll get started working with Git by setting your defaults and preferences, and learn the basics of creating a repository and adding initial content to it.

Basic Configuration

Before starting in with Git, you'll want to set a few basic parameters using `git config`. This command reads and changes Git configuration at the repository, personal, or system level. Your personal Git configuration is in *~/.gitconfig*; this is a plain-text file, which you can edit directly as well, if you like. Its format is called *INI style* (after a file extension commonly used for it, though not by Git), and is divided into sections, like so:

```
[user]
        name = Richard E. Silverman

[color]
        ui = auto # overall default for color usage

[mergetool "ediff"]
        trustExitCode = true
```

Comments are introduced with a hash sign (#) as shown, as is common in Unix configuration files. The parameters have full names qualified by the section in which they appear using a dot; for example, the parameters mentioned in this example are:

- `user.name`
- `color.ui`
- `mergetool.ediff.trustExitCode`

You use these names when reading or setting parameters with `git config`, rather than editing the file yourself. To set a parameter with `git config`:

```
$ git config --{local,global,system} parameter value
```

If you give this command when your current directory is inside a Git repository, it implies `--local`, and it will change the configuration for that repository only, in the file *.git/config*. Otherwise, the default is `--global`, which applies to your overall personal Git configuration in *~/.gitconfig*. The `--system` option changes the system-wide configuration on the machine you're logged into, which applies to all users; its location may vary, but is usually */etc/gitconfig*. This file is usually writable only by a system administrator, so you'd need to be root to run this command to make a change. It's not common to do that anyway; usually this file would be maintained separately, perhaps using a configuration management system such as Puppet (*https://puppet labs.com/*) or Chef (*http://www.opscode.com/chef/*).

Git reads these three configurations, each if available, in the order system, global, then local. Settings made in a later configuration override those from an earlier one so that, for example, you can set your normal email address with `--global` but change it for commits made in a specific repository if you use a different address when corresponding about that work.

Parameters that take Boolean (yes/no) values can be given as `yes`/`no`, `true`/`false`, or `on`/`off`.

See *git-config(1)* for more detail on the format of the configuration files, its many parameters (some mentioned in this text and some not), and other uses of git config, such as querying the current setting of a parameter.

Personal Identification

Git will guess your name and email address from the environment, but those may vary from one computer to another and may not be what you want. To set them:

```
$ git config --global user.name "Richard E. Silverman"
$ git config --global user.email res@oreilly.com
```

If you use the same *~/.gitconfig* in multiple contexts, say at home and at work, then this may be inconvenient. Git will take your email address from the EMAIL environment variable before resorting to a guess, so you can leave it out of your Git configuration and set EMAIL appropriately in the different contexts, usually with your shell startup files, such as *.bashrc*, *.profile*, *.cshrc*, and so on. There are other environment variables for finer control as well, such as GIT_AUTHOR_NAME and GIT_COMMITTER_EMAIL; these refer to the fact that Git maintains a distinction between the author of a change and the person who committed it. See *git-commit-tree(1)* for details, as well as "Defining Your Own Formats" on page 130.

Text Editor

When you use git commit, you supply some free-form text, which is included in the commit; this is the "commit message." You can give this on the command line with the -m switch, but you can also use your favorite text editor to compose the message instead. If you omit the -m switch, Git starts a text editor to let you write your message. The default editor varies by platform; on Unix, it is the ubiquitous *vi*. You can customize this with the environment variables GIT_EDITOR, EDITOR, or VISUAL (the latter two are respected by many other Unix programs as well), or by setting core.editor. For example (reflecting the author's predilections):

```
$ git config --global core.editor emacs
```

Git uses the first of these variables it finds in the order given.

Commit ID Abbreviation

When referring directly to an object identifier, it is usually not necessary to quote the entire 40-character hexadecimal SHA-1 value; any initial substring unique to the current context will do. You can tell Git to abbreviate commit IDs generally with:

```
$ git config --global log.abbrevCommit yes
$ git config --global core.abbrev 8
```

This improves readability in various places, especially in log output such as:

```
$ git log --pretty=oneline
222433ee Update draft release notes to 1.7.10
2fa91bd3 Merge branch 'maint'
70eb1307 Documentation: do not assume that n -> 1 in …
...
```

where the commit messages would otherwise be pushed halfway off the screen to the right by the full identifiers. core.abbrev is the length of the shortened identifiers in digits; the default is 7 in most cases. To see the full identifiers as a per-command exception, use --no-abbrev-commit. Note that when you're quoting commit IDs in a public or "for the record" context, it may be best to use the full ID, to avoid any future ambiguities.

Pagination

Git will automatically pipe output from many commands such as git log and git status to *less(1)* for pagination; you can select a different program with the core.pager variable (or the environment variable GIT_PAGER), and disable pagination entirely by setting this to be simply cat (or something equivalently transparent). You can control pagination on a per-command basis by setting a Boolean pager.*command*, e.g., pager.status for git status (this can also be the name of the pager program to use for this specific command). You may also want to read the *git-config(1)* section on core.pager, which discusses specific things Git does with the LESS environment variable to affect the behavior of *less(1)*.

Color

Many Git commands, including `diff`, `log`, and `branch`, can use color to help you interpret their output, but these options are mostly off by default. To enable the use of color generally, set:

```
$ git config --global color.ui auto
```

(`ui` stands for "user interface.") This will turn on most color options when Git is talking to a terminal (tty/pty device). You can then turn off color for individual commands if you prefer; for example, to disable it for `git branch` (but leave it on for other functions):

```
$ git config --global color.branch no
```

Git's use of color is very configurable, down to defining new color names, specifying terminal control sequences, and using color in custom log formats. See *git-config(1)* and *git-log(1)* for details.

Cryptographic Keys

Git can use GnuPG (*http://www.gnupg.org/*) ("gpg") to cryptographically sign tags and commits in order to verify the authenticity of sensitive assertions such as, "This tagged commit contains the version 3.0 source code." See "git tag" on page 191 for more on signing tags. By default, Git passes your name and email address to GnuPG to select the signing key. If the combination of your Git and GnuPG settings doesn't select the correct key, you can set it explicitly with:

```
$ git config --global user.signingkey 6B4FB2D0
```

You can use any key identifier GnuPG supports; `6B4FB2D0` happens to be an ID for the author's personal key. You can also use one of the email addresses bound to the key you want, if it's unique among your keys.

Command Aliases

Most systems provide a way to abbreviate long commands with user-defined command aliases; for instance, using `alias` in your Unix *bash* shell startup file *~/.bashrc*. Git has its own internal alias system as well, which may be more convenient. This command:

```
$ git config --global alias.cp cherry-pick
```

defines `git cp` as an alias for `git cherry-pick`. An exclamation point means to pass the alias definition to the shell, letting you use more complex aliases; for example, this definition in *~/.git-config*:

```
[alias]
    setup = ! "git init; git add .; git commit"
```

defines an alias `git setup`, which sets up a new repository using the contents of the current directory.

More generally, whenever you type `git something`, if `something` is not a built-in command or defined alias, Git searches its installation path (often */usr/lib/git-core*) and then your own search path for a program named `git-something`. So, you can make your own Git command `git foo` just by placing a program in an executable file named *git-foo* somewhere on your personal path (usually, the value of the `PATH` environment variable).

Getting Help

You can get help with a Git command or feature using Git itself, for example:

```
$ git help commit
```

This displays the documentation for the command `git commit`. On Unix systems, this documentation is available via the usual man page system as well; this is equivalent:

```
$ man git-commit
```

References

- *git-init(1)*
- *git-commit-tree(1)*
- *git-config(1)*
- *git-log(1)* ["Pretty Formats"]

Creating a New, Empty Repository

The command:

```
$ git init directory
```

creates the argument directory if needed, and a directory named *.git* inside it holding a new, empty Git repository. Aside from the repository itself in *.git*, that directory will hold the *working tree*: copies of the files and directories under version control that you will edit. The *.git* directory holds the files and data structures that form the repository itself, including the database of all historical revisions of all project files. Unlike CVS and (until recently) Subversion, there is no control directory in each directory of the working tree (*CVS* and *.svn*); there is just the one *.git* directory at the top of the project tree.

The default with no argument is the current directory; that is, a simple git init creates a new *.git* in the current directory.

git init is a safe command. It will not remove any existing files in the target directory, the usual pattern being that you are about to add those files to the new repository. It will also not damage an existing repository, even though it gives a somewhat heart-stopping message about "reinitializing" if you do it; all this actually does is make some administrative updates, such as picking up new templates for "hook" scripts made available by the system administrator (see "Git Hooks" on page 196).

Selected Options

`--bare`

> Creates a "bare" repository; that is, one without an associated working tree. The internal repository files that would otherwise be inside *.git* are instead created in the target directory itself, and certain repository options are set differently, principally `core.bare = yes`. A bare repository usually serves as a point of coordination for a centralized workflow, in which several people push and pull from that repository rather than directly among themselves; no one works with the bare copy directly.

`--shared`

> Sets group ownership, file permissions, and options to support multiple Unix accounts pushing into a non-bare repository. The normal expectation is that if someone wants to send you an update to a project you're both working on, she will ask you to pull from her repository, so that one way or another you are the only person who ever actually modifies your repository. The usual file permissions reflect this, allowing only you to modify the repository files. The `--shared` option arranges permissions to allow others in a common Unix group to push directly into your repository, as well as pull from it. There are several settings for this option, manipulating the details of group ownership, file permissions, interactions with people's umask settings, and so on; see *git-init(1)* for details.
>
> This arrangement isn't much used, though; ordinarily you and your coworker would simply pull from one another's repositories into your own, or push to a shared bare repository. Pushing into a nonbare repository is awkward, because it will fail if you try to push the branch that is currently checked out in the remote (since that could invalidate the remote's working tree and index at any moment). A bare repository doesn't have a working tree or index (since no one is using it directly), and so does not have this limitation.

THE .git DIRECTORY

Though the repository is usually stored in a directory named *.git* at the top of the working tree, there are ways to locate it elsewhere: you can use `git --git-dir` *directory* to refer explicitly to another loction, or set the environment variable `GIT_DIR`. For simplicity and to match the common case, we will generally just refer to *.git* when talking about the repository directory.

Importing an Existing Project

These commands create a new repository and add all content in the current directory to it:

```
$ git init
$ git add .
$ git commit -m 'Begin Project Foo!'
```

To illustrate:

```
$ cd hello
$ ls -l
total 12
-rw-r----- 1 res  res   50 Mar  4 19:54 README
-rw-r----- 1 res  res  127 Mar  4 19:53 hello.c
-rw-r----- 1 res  res   27 Mar  4 19:53 hello.h
$ git init
Initialized empty Git repository in /u/res/hello/.git/
$ git add .
$ git commit -m 'Begin Project Foo!'
[master (root-commit) cb9c236f] Begin Project Foo!
3 files changed, 13 insertions(+)
create mode 100644 README
create mode 100644 hello.c
create mode 100644 hello.h
```

This creates a new Git repository *.git* in the current directory, and adds the contents of the entire directory tree rooted there to the repository as the initial commit on a new branch named *master:*

```
$ git branch
* master
$ git log --stat
commit cb9c236f
Author: Richard E. Silverman <res@oreilly.com>
Date:   Sun Mar 4 19:57:45 2012 -0500
Begin Project Foo!
README  |   3 +++
hello.c |   7 +++++++
hello.h |   3 +++
3 files changed, 13 insertions(+)
```

In more detail: git add . adds the current directory to the (initially empty) index; this includes files as well as directories and their contents, and so on, recursively. git commit then creates a new tree object capturing the current state of the index, as well as a commit object with your comment text, personal identification, the current time, and so on, pointing to that tree. It records these in the object database, and then finally sets the *master* branch to the new commit; that is, makes the ref refs/heads/master point to the new commit ID:

```
$ git log --pretty=oneline
cb9c236f Begin Project Foo!
$ git show-ref master
cb9c236f refs/heads/master
```

git log shows the ID of the most recent (and right now only) commit, and git show-ref master shows the commit ID currently referred to by the branch *master;* you can see that they are the same.

Ignoring Files

While you're working on a project, you may have files in your working directory that you want Git to simply ignore. If it's a small project in an interpreted language, this may not happen so much, but it's definitely an issue for projects that produce compiled code of any sort, or use tools like *autoconf*, or generate documentation automatically in various formats. Such files include:

object code
>*.o, *.so, *.a, *.dll, *.exe*

bytecode
>*.jar* (Java), *.elc* (Emacs Lisp), *.pyc* (Python)

toolchain artifacts
>*config.log, config.status, aclocal.m4, Makefile.in, config.h*

Generally speaking, anything that is automatically generated you probably don't want tracked by Git, and you don't want Git constantly including them in listings or complaining about them either. Git looks at three different kinds of files to determine what to ignore, in order:

1. Files named *.gitignore* in your working tree. This is just another file to Git as far as content is concerned—it will list it as "untracked" if it's present but not in the repository—and so you normally add it to the repository content; thus, if this is shared work, you should only put things there that make sense for other people to ignore as well. You can actually put `.gitignore` in a *.gitignore* file, and cause it to ignore itself. All *.gitignore* files in the current and containing directories in the repository are read, with rules in files closer to the current directory overriding those in files farther away.

2. The per-repository file *.git/info/exclude*. This is part of your repository configuration, but not part of the repository content, so unlike a tracked *.gitignore* file, it is not automatically foisted upon people who clone your project. This is a good place to put things you find convenient to ignore for this project, but about which others might disagree (or if you simply decide not to use *.gitignore* files as a matter of policy, to avoid confusion).

3. A file named by the configuration variable `core.excludes file`, if you set it. You might do this:

```
$ git config --global core.excludesfile ~/.gitignore
```

and keep a set of ignore patterns there that you want Git to always observe. That's assuming your home directory is not itself inside a Git repository, of course, in which case you might want to name the file something else (and ask yourself if you don't perhaps like Git just a bit too much).

Syntax of "Ignore Patterns"

See *gitignore(5)* for precise details; generally speaking, an ignore file uses shell "glob" patterns and comments in the following fashion. Note the use of the exclamation point to introduce a negated pattern, overriding subcases of an earlier pattern. Git reads all patterns in a file to determine the disposition of a given path, rather than stopping at the first match, and the last matching line is the one that applies:

```
# Ignore this specific file in a subdirectory.
conf/config.h

# Ignore this specific file in the current directory.
# (not "./")
/super-cool-program

## Patterns without slashes apply everywhere in this
## directory and below.

# Ignore individual objects and object archives
# (*.o and *.a).
*.[oa]

# Ignore shared objects...
*.so

# ... but don't ignore this file, or my boyfriend
# will complain.
!my.so

# Ignore any directories named "temp," but still
# notice regular files and symbolic links with
# that name.
temp/
```

In *.git/info/exclude* or your *core.excludesfile*, the "current directory" indicated earlier is the top of the working tree.

Note that all this applies only to untracked files; you cannot tell Git to ignore changes to a tracked file this way. The command `git update-index --assume-unchanged` is useful for that.

NOTE

Shell "globs" are simple patterns, not as powerful as regular expressions; Git uses them to indicate sets of files and refs. There are many slightly different versions of the glob syntax, as it has been around for a long time; the one used in Git is documented in the *fnmatch(3)* and *glob(3)* man pages. Simply put: `*` matches a sequence of characters not containing `/`; `?` matches a single character (again not `/`); and `[abc]` matches one character, which must be either `a`, `b`, or `c`.

## CHAPTER 3

Making Commits

This chapter explains how to make changes to your repository content: add, edit, and remove files; manipulate the index; and commit changes.

Changing the Index

When you run `git commit`, without arguments or options, Git adds the contents of the index as a new commit on the current branch. So before committing, you add to the index those changes you want to commit. This can skip some changes you've made to your working files, if you're not ready to commit those yet.

---

git commit <FILENAME>

Giving a specific filename to `git commit` works differently: it ignores the index, and commits just the changes to that file.

Adding a New File

```
$ git add filename
```

This is suitably mnemonic, but note the next command.

Adding the Changes to an Existing File

```
$ git add filename
```

Yes, this is the same command. In both cases, Git adds the current working file contents to the object database as a new blob-type object (assuming it's not already there), and notes the change in the index. If the file is new, then this will be a new index entry; if not, just an updated one pointing to the new object (or with changed attributes, such as permissions)—but it's essentially the same operation to Git. A file is "new" if its pathname is not in the index, usually meaning it was not part of the last commit; this is what causes git status to note a file as "untracked" prior to your adding it (files in the index are called "tracked," and they are the ones Git cares about, generally speaking).

The filename can be a directory, in which case Git adds all new files and changes to tracked files under that directory.

Adding Partial Changes

```
$ git add -p
```

You can also add only *some* of the changes you've made to a file, using git add --patch (-p). This starts an interactive loop in which you can select portions of the changes you've made and skip others. When you're done, Git adds to the index versions of the relevant files with only those changes applied to them. git status reports this situation by listing the same file under both "changes not staged for commit" *and* "changes to be committed," since the file now has a mix of both.

This is an important feature, since it helps you to make well-factored commits. When you're done with some editing and ready to commit, you may realize that you've made changes that ought to be represented by more than one commit; perhaps you've fixed two bugs in the same file, or tidied up some unrelated comments while you were at it. git add -p allows you to conveniently split the work up into separate commits.

The interactive loop has a number of options with integrated help (use "?"), but note particularly the s command to split a set of changes, called a "hunk," into smaller changes (if Git's initial analysis glues together pieces you want separated), and the e command, which allows you to edit hunks yourself. If you set the interactive.singlekey Git configuration variable, you can use single keystrokes for these commands and skip typing return after each.

Just running git add -p with no arguments will let you examine all files with unstaged changes (unlike just git add, which requires an argument or option to tell it what to add). You can also specify particular files to consider as arguments.

git add -p is actually a special case of git add --interactive (-i). The latter starts at a higher level, allowing you to view status, add untracked files, revert to the HEAD version, select files to patch, etc.; git add -p just jumps straight to the "patch" sub-command of git add -i.

Shortcuts

git add -u
> Include all files in the current index; this includes changed and deleted files, but not new ones.

git add -A
> Include all filenames in the index and in the working tree; this stages new files as well. This is useful if you are importing a new version of code from another source not in Git, traditionally called a "vendor branch." You would replace your working tree with the unpacked new code, then use git add -A to stage all changes, additions, and deletions necessary to commit the new version. Add -f to include normally ignored files.

Removing a File

```
$ git rm filename
```

This does two things:

1. Deletes the file's entry from the index, scheduling it for removal in the next commit

2. Deletes the working file as well, as with `rm filename`

If you happen to delete the working file yourself first, that's no problem; Git won't care. Removing it from the index is what matters; deleting the working copy afterward is just being tidy. In both cases, `git status` will show the file as deleted; the difference will be whether it is listed under "changes not staged for commit" (if you just deleted the working file), or "changes to be committed" (if you used `git rm`).

`git rm` on a file not yet under version control won't work, though; just use `rm`.

Renaming a File

Renaming a file or moving a directory in Git is simple, using the `git mv` command:

```
$ git mv foo bar
```

This is actually just a shortcut for renaming the working file outside Git, then using `git add` on the new name:

```
$ mv foo bar
$ git add bar
```

Renaming is a thorny topic in version control generally. Renaming a file is in a sense equivalent to deleting that file and creating a new one with a different name and the same contents—but that might also occur without your meaning to rename anything, if the new file just happens to coincide with the old one. The distinction is one of intent, and so must be represented separately by the system if it is to be captured at all. And it can be quite important to do so, because people generally want the history of a renamed file to be preserved; by even calling what we've done "renaming," we are implicitly saying that this is really "the same file, just with a different name." We don't want to lose the history just because we changed the name. Which begs the question: just what is a "file," anyway? Is it just the content? No, because we track changes to content to the same file over time. Is it just the name? No, because sometimes we want to "rename" the file, which considers the content to be primary and the name secondary. The truth is that there is no single answer to this question, since it depends on the user's wishes in a particular situation—and so it is hard to design a single system to accommodate it, and systems vary in how they do so. CVS does not handle renaming at all. Subversion has explicit renaming: it represents a rename operation separately from a delete/create pair. This has some advantages, but also engenders considerable complexity in the system to support it.

Git's approach is to not track renaming explicitly, but rather to infer it from combinations of name and content changes; content-based addressing makes this particularly easy and attractive as a matter of implementation. Git doesn't have a "rename" function internally at all; as indicated, `git mv` is just a shortcut. If you run `git status` after the first command earlier, you'll see what you'd expect: Git shows *foo* as deleted, and the new file *bar* as untracked. If you do it after the `git add`, though, you see just one annotation: `renamed: foo -> bar`. Git sees that the file for a particular index entry has been removed from disk, while a new entry has appeared with a different filename—but the *same object ID*, and hence the same contents. It can also consider renaming relative to a less strict notion of file equivalence —that is, if a new file is sufficiently similar to one that's been deleted rather than 100% identical (see the options for renaming and copy detection in Chapter 9).

This approach is very simple, but it requires that you sometimes be aware of the mechanics. For example: because this analysis is expensive, it is turned off by default when examining history with `git log`; you have to remember to enable it with `-M` if you want to see renaming. Also, if you edit a file substantially *and* rename it in a single commit, it may not show up as a rename at all; you're better off editing, committing, then doing the rename in a separate commit to make sure it shows up as such.

Unstaging Changes

If you want to start over with this process, it's easy: just use `git reset`. This resets the index to match the current commit, undoing any changes you've made with `git add`. `git reset` reports the files with outstanding changes after its action:

```
$ git reset
Unstaged changes after reset:
M       old-and-busted.c
M       new-hotness.hs
```

You can also give specific files or directories to reset, leaving staged changes in other files alone. With `git reset --patch` you can be even more specific, interactively selecting portions of your staged changes to unstage; it is the reverse of `git add -p`. See "Discarding Any Number of Commits" on page 61 for other options.

Making a Commit

When you've prepared the index you want, use `git commit` to store it as a new commit. Use `git status` first to check the files involved, and `git diff --cached` to check the actual changes you're applying. `git diff` alone shows any remaining *unstaged* changes (the difference between your working tree and the index); adding `--cached` (or the synonym `--staged`) shows the difference between the index and the last commit instead (i.e., the changes you're about to make with this commit).

Commit Messages

Each commit has an associated "commit message": some free-form text used to describe the changes introduced by that commit. You can give the message on the command line as:

```
$ git commit -m "an interesting commit message"
```

If you don't, Git will start a text editor to allow you to enter your message; "Text Editor" on page 35 describes how the editor is chosen. Although the text is free-form, the usual practice is to make the first line no longer than 50–60 characters or so. If you need further lines, then separate them from the first one with a blank line, and wrap the remaining paragraphs to 72 characters. The first line should serve as a subject line for the commit, as with an email. The intention is to allow listings that include the commit message to usefully abbreviate the message with its first line, still leaving space for some other information on the line (e.g., `git log --oneline`).

It's actually rather important to follow this convention, since lots of Git-related software as well as various parts of Git itself assume it. The subject line of a commit is addressable as a separate entity when writing commit formats and extracting commit information, and programs that display commits in various contexts assume that the subject will make sense on its own and not be too long. GitHub and *gitweb* both do this visually, for example, displaying the subject as a separate item in bold at the top, with the rest of the message (the "body"), if any, set in smaller text below. You'll get odd-looking results that are difficult to read if the first line is just a sentence fragment and/or too long to fit in the allotted space.

Following this convention can also help you make better commits: if you find it difficult to summarize the changes, consider whether they might better be split into separate commits—which brings up the topic of the next section.

What Makes a Good Commit?

This depends on how you intend to use your repository and Git in general; there's no single right answer to this question. Some people use the convention (if the content is software) that every commit must be buildable, which means that commits will generally be larger since they must contain everything required to advance the code from one coherent stage to another. Another approach is to structure your commits primarily to take advantage of Git's ability to transmit and reuse them. When preparing a commit, ask yourself: does it contain entirely and only the changes necessary to do what the commit message says it does?

If the commit says it implements a feature, does someone using git cherry-pick to try out the feature have a decent chance of that succeeding, or does the commit also contain unrelated changes that will complicate this? Think also about later using git revert to undo a change, or about merging this branch into other branches to incorporate the new feature. In this style, each commit might not produce functional software, since it could make sense to represent a large overall change as a series of commits in order to better reuse its parts. You can use other methods to indicate larger project checkpoints like buildable intermediate versions, including Git tags or unique strings in commit messages, which you can find using git log --grep.

Be careful too with the timing of your commits, as well as with their content. If you are going to make wide-ranging, disruptive changes such as adjusting whitespace, renaming functions or variables, or changing indentation, you should do that at a time when others can conveniently take your changes as given, since automatic merge is likely to fail miserably in such cases. Doing these things while others are doing lots of work on related branches—say, when a big merge is coming up—will make that merge a nightmare.

There are other issues about which version control users in general can argue endlessly: for example, how should commit messages be phrased grammatically? Some like the imperative mood ("fix a bug"), while others favor the past tense ("fixed a bug"). It is common in the Git source code itself to refer to adding a feature as "teaching Git" to do something. Obviously there is no strict guideline to be had here, though consistency at least makes it easier to search for specific changes.

Shortcuts

git commit -a adds all tracked, modified files to the index before committing. This commits changed and deleted files, but not new ones; it is equivalent to git add -u followed by git commit. Be careful, though; if you get too accustomed to using this command, you may accidentally commit some changes you didn't intend to—though that's easy to undo; see the next chapter.

Empty Directories

Git does not track directories as separate entities; rather, it creates directories in the working tree as needed to create the paths to files it checks out, and removes directories if there are no longer any files in them. This implies that you can't represent an empty directory directly to Git; you have to put at least one placeholder file within the directory to get Git to create it.

A Commit Workflow

Here's a procedure for making multiple commits from a single set of edits to your working files, while making sure each commit is good:

1. Use `git add` (with various options) to stage a subset of your changes.

2. Run `git stash --keep-index`. This saves and undoes your outstanding, unstaged changes while preserving your staged changes in the index, and resets your working tree to match the index.

3. Examine this working tree state to make sure your selection of changes makes sense; build and test your software, for example.

4. Run `git commit`.

5. Now, use `git stash pop` to restore your remaining unstaged changes, and go back to step 1. Continue this process until you've committed all your changes, as confirmed by `git status` reporting "nothing to commit, working directory clean."

See "git stash" on page 188 for more on the useful `git stash` command.

## CHAPTER 4

Undoing and Editing Commits

In Chapter 3, we discussed staging changes in the index for inclusion in the next commit. This chapter is about undoing or correcting changes once you've committed them.

With centralized version control, committing and publishing a change are the same thing: as soon as you commit to the shared repository, others can see and start using your changes. This makes undoing a commit problematic; how do you retract a commit others have already checked out or merged?

With Git, however, this is not a problem, since you are committing to your own private repository. You are free to delete or change your local commits as you please, and Git gives you the tools to do that; publishing those commits is a separate action, via pushing to shared repository or asking others to pull from yours.

Changing already published commits is awkward, of course, since it would cause others to lose history they already have; Git will warn people pulling from you of that, and you might not even be allowed to push such changes to a shared repository. The extra step afforded by Git is crucial, though: by separating committing and publishing, it allows you to use version control freely for your own purposes as you work, then clean up your commits for public consumption before publishing them.

Note that most of the techniques discussed in this chapter only make sense when the portion of history involved is linear; that is, contains no merge commits. We will discuss techniques for editing a branched history in Chapter 10.

NOTE

Technically, you can't "change" a commit. Because of content-based addressing, if you change anything about a commit, it becomes a different commit, since it now has a different object ID. So when we speak of changing a commit, we really mean replacing it with one having corrected attributes or contents. But since the intention is to change the history, it's convenient to use this phrasing, and we'll do so.

Changing the Last Commit

The most common correction to make is to the previous commit: you run git commit, and then realize you made a mistake—perhaps you forgot to include a new file, or left out some comments. This common situation is also the easiest one to address. There's no preparatory step; just make whatever corrections you need, adding these to the index as usual. Then use this command:

```
$ git commit --amend
```

Git will present you with the previous commit message to edit if you like; then, it simply discards the previous commit and puts a new one in its place, with your corrections. You can add -C HEAD if you want to reuse the previous commit message as-is.

The --amend feature is a good example of how Git's internal organization makes many operations very easy, both to implement and to understand. The tip commit on the current branch has a pointer to the previous commit, its parent; that is all that links it to the rest of the branch. In particular, no commits point *to* this one, so no other commits are affected (recall that commits point to their parents, but not to their children). Thus, discarding the tip commit consists only of moving the branch pointer backward to the previous one; nothing else need be done. Eventually, if the discarded commit remains disconnected from the commit graph, Git will delete it from the object database as part of periodic garbage collection.

Having dropped the previous commit, the repository state you want to change and re-commit would appear to be lost...but no: there's another copy of it in the index, since that commit was made from the current index. So you simply modify the index as desired, and commit again.

Although we described it in terms of a linear history, `git commit --amend` works with merge commits as well; then there are multiple parents and branches involved instead of just one, but it operates analogously.

FIXING A COMMIT MESSAGE

If you use `git commit --amend` without making any changes to the index, Git still allows you to edit the commit message if you like, or you can give the new message with the `-m` option. This still requires replacing the last commit, since the message text is part of the commit; the new commit will just have the same content (point to the same tree) as the previous one.

Double Oops!

Suppose you're having an off day and, having committed and then amended that commit, you suddenly realize that you just lost some information from the first commit that you didn't mean to. You would appear to be out of luck: that commit has been discarded, and unless you happen to have its object ID, you have no way to refer to it, even though it's still in the object database. Git has a feature to save you, though, called the *reflog*:

```
$ git log -g
```

The `git log` command, which we will discuss in Chapter 9, normally shows the history of your project via portions of the commit graph. The `-g` option shows something entirely different, however. For each branch, Git maintains a log of operations performed while on that branch, called its "reflog." Recall that a branch is just a ref pointing to the tip commit of the branch; each ref can have a log recording its referents over time. `git log -g` displays a composite reflog, starting with the current branch and chaining back through commands that switch branches, such as `git checkout`. For example:

```
$ git log -g
e674ab77 HEAD@{0}: commit (amend): Digital Restrictio…
965dfda4 HEAD@{1}: commit: Digital Rights Management
dd31deb3 HEAD@{2}: commit: Mozart
3307465c HEAD@{3}: commit: Beethoven
6273a3b0 HEAD@{4}: merge topic: Fast-forward
d77b78fa HEAD@{5}: checkout: moving from sol to master
6273a3b0 HEAD@{6}: commit: amalthea
2ee20b94 HEAD@{7}: pull: Merge made by the 'recursive…
d77b78fa HEAD@{8}: checkout: moving from master to sol
1ad385f2 HEAD@{9}: commit (initial): Anfang
```

The reflog shows the sequence of operations performed: `commit`, `pull`, `checkout`, `merge`, etc. The notation *branch@{n}* refers to a numbered entry in the reflog for *branch*; in this case HEAD, the current branch. The crucial thing for us, though, is the first column of object IDs: each one names the commit that was the branch tip after the operation on that line was completed. Thus, when I made the commit for entry #1 in this reflog, with the comment "Digital Rights Management," the branch moved to commit 965dfda4, which means this is the ID for that commit. After I used `git commit --amend` to fix the commit message, the branch looked like this:

```
$ git log
e674ab77 Digital Restrictions Management
dd31deb3 Mozart
3307465c Beethoven
...
```

Commit 965dfda4 is absent, removed from the history, but the reflog retains a record of it. You can use `git show 965dfda4` to view the diff for that commit and recover the missing information, or `git checkout 965dfda4` to move your working tree to that state, if that's more convenient.

See "Names Relative to the Reflog" on page 118 for more about the reflog.

Discarding the Last Commit

Suppose you make a commit, but then decide that you weren't ready to do that. You don't have a specific fix to make, as with `git commit --amend`; you just want to "uncommit" and continue working. This is simple; just do:

```
$ git reset HEAD~
Unstaged changes after reset:
M       Zeus
M       Adonis
```

`git reset` is a versatile command, with several modes and actions. It always moves the head of the current branch to a given commit, but differs in how it treats the working tree and index; in this usage, it updates the index but leaves the working tree alone. The HEAD ref refers to the tip of current branch as always, and the trailing tilde names the commit prior to that one (see Chapter 8). Thus, the effect of this command is to move the branch back one commit, discarding the latest one (but you can still recover it via reflog, as before). Since it also resets the index to match, any corresponding changes in your working tree are now unstaged again, which Git reports as shown along with any other outstanding changes (the M is for "modified"; it may also show A for "added," D for "deleted," and so on).

Discarding Any Number of Commits

In the foregoing description, the only thing limiting the action to "the last commit" is the expression HEAD~; it works just as well to discard any number of consecutive commits at the end of a branch. This action is sometimes called "rewinding the branch." For example, to discard three commits resetting the branch tip to the fourth commit back, do:

```
$ git reset HEAD~3
```

HEAD~3 refers to the fourth commit back, because this numbering syntax starts at zero; HEAD and HEAD~0 are equivalent.

When discarding more than one commit, some further options to git reset become useful:

--mixed
> The default: makes the index match the given commit, but does not change the working files. Changes made since the last commit appear unstaged.

--soft
> This resets the branch tip only, and does not change the index; the discarded commit's changes remain staged. You might use this to stage all the changes from several previous commits, and then reapply them as a single commit.

--merge
> Tries to keep your outstanding file changes while rewinding the branch, where this makes sense: files with unstaged changes are kept, while files differing between HEAD and the given commit are updated. If there is overlap between those sets, the reset fails.

--hard
> Resets your working files to match the given commit, as well as the index. Any changes you've made since the discarded commit are permanently lost, so be careful with this option! Resist the urge to make an alias or shortcut for using git reset --hard; you will probably regret it.

Undoing a Commit

Suppose you want to undo the effect of an earlier commit—you don't want to edit the history to do this, but rather make a new

---

commit undoing the earlier commit's changes. The command
git revert makes this easy; just give it the commit you want to
undo:

```
$ git revert 9c6a1fad
```

This will compute the diff between that commit and the previous
one, reverse it, and then attempt to apply that to your working
tree (you may have merge conflicts to resolve if intervening
changes complicate doing that automatically). Git will prepare a
commit message indicating the commit being reverted and its
subject, which you can edit.

Partial Undo

If you only want to undo some of the changes from an earlier
commit, you can use a combination of commands we've seen
before:

```
$ git revert -n commit
$ git reset
$ git add -p
$ git commit
$ git checkout .
```

The -n option to git revert tells Git to apply and stage the reverted changes, but stop short of making a commit. You then
unstage all the changes with git reset, and restage only those
you want using the interactive git add -p. Finally, after committing the subset of changes you want, you discard the rest by
checking out the contents of the index, overwriting the remaining
applied changes from git revert.

Plain git revert will complain if you have staged changes in the
index (that is, the index does not match the HEAD commit), since
its purpose is to make a new commit based on the one to be
reverted, and it would lose your changes if it reset the index in
order to do that. git revert -n, though, will *not* complain about
that, since it is *not* making a commit.

Note that if the commit you're reverting deleted a file, then this
will add it back. After git reset though, the recovered file will

appear as "untracked" to Git, and `git add -p` will not see it; you'll have to add it again separately, if it's one of the changes you want to make (`git add --interactive (-i)` can help with that; it's more general, and `git add -p` is actually a commonly used subcommand of it). Similarly, the final checkout will not remove a restored file that you chose not to add; you'll have to remove it yourself. You can use `git reset --hard` or `git clean`, but be careful not to accidentally remove other untracked files or revert other working tree changes you may have.

Editing a Series of Commits

`git commit --amend` is nice, but what if you want to change a commit that is now a few steps back in your history? Since each commit refers to the one preceding it, changing one means all the following commits must be replaced, even if you don't need to make any other changes to them. The `--amend` feature works as simply as it does precisely because there are no following commits to consider.

In fact, Git allows you to edit any linear sequence of commits leading up to a branch tip—not only with regard to their messages and contents, but also to rearrange them, remove some, collapse some together or split some into further commits. The feature to use is `git rebase`. Rebasing is a general technique intended to move a branch from one location to another, and we will consider it more fully in "Rebasing" on page 149. While moving a branch, however, it also lets you use a very general "sequence editor" to transform the branch at the same time (with the option `--interactive (-i)`), and that is the feature we want here. This command:

```
$ git rebase -i HEAD~n
```

rewrites the last *n* commits on the current branch. It does in fact ask Git to "move" the branch, but the destination is the same as the starting point, so the branch location does not actually change, and you get to use the sequence editor to alter commits as you like in the process.

In response to this command, Git starts your editor and presents a one-line description of each commit in the range indicated, like so:

```
# action commit-ID subject
pick 51090ce fix bug #1234
pick 15f4720 edit man pages for spelling and grammar
pick 9b0e3dc add prototypes for the 'frobnitz' module
pick 583bb4e fix null pointer (We are not strong.)
pick 45a9484 update README
```

Watch out: the order here is that in which the commits were made (and in which they will be remade), which is generally the *opposite* of what you would see from git log, which uses reverse chronological order (most recent commit first).

Now edit the first column, the action, to tell Git what you want to do with each commit. The available actions are:

pick

Use the commit as-is. Git will not stop for this commit unless there is a conflict.

reword

Change just the commit message. Git allows you to edit the message before reapplying this commit.

edit

Change the commit contents (and message, if you want). Here, Git stops after remaking this commit and allows you to do whatever you want. The usual thing is to use git commit --amend to replace the commit, then git rebase --continue to let Git continue with the rebase operation. However, you could also insert further commits, perhaps splitting the original changes up into several smaller commits. Git simply picks up from where you leave off, with the next change you asked it to make.

squash

Make this commit's changes part of the preceding one. To meld several consecutive commits into one, leave the first one marked pick and mark the remaining ones with squash. Git concatenates all the commit messages for you to edit.

fixup
> Like squash, but discard the message of this commit when composing the composite message.

You can abbreviate an action to just its initial letter, such as r for reword. You can also reorder the lines to make the new commits in a different order, or remove a commit entirely by deleting its line. If you want to cancel the rebase, just save a file with no action lines; Git will abort if it finds nothing to do. It will *not* abort if you just leave the directions as you found them, but the result will be the same in this simple case, since Git will find it does not need to remake any commits in order to follow the directions (which say to use each commit as-is with pick). At any point when Git stops, you can abort the entire process and return to your previous state with git rebase --abort.

Conflicts

It's possible to ask for changes that invalidate the existing commits. For example: if one commit adds a file and a later commit changes that file, and you reverse the order of these commits, then Git cannot apply the new first patch, since it says to alter a file that doesn't yet exist. Also, patches to existing files rely on context, which may change if you edit the contents of earlier commits. In this case, Git will stop, indicate the problem, and ask you to resolve the conflict before proceeding. For example:

```
error: could not apply fcff9f72... (commit message)

When you have resolved this problem, run "git rebase
--continue".  If you prefer to skip this patch, run
"git rebase --skip" instead.  To check out the
original branch and stop rebasing, run "git rebase
--abort".

Could not apply fcff9f7... (commit message)
```

Here, Git uses the same mechanism for indicating conflicts as when performing a merge; see "Merge Conflicts" on page 98 for details on how to examine and resolve them. When you're done, as indicated above, just run `git rebase --continue` to make the now-repaired commit, and move on to the next edit.

TIP

When you ask to edit a commit, Git stops *after* making the commit, and you use `git commit --amend` to replace it before going on. When there's a conflict, however, Git cannot make all the requested changes, so it stops *before* making the commit (having made and staged whatever changes it can, and marked the conflicts for you to resolve). When you continue after resolving the conflicts, Git will then make the current commit. You do not commit yourself or use the --amend feature when fixing a conflict.

The exec Action

There is actually another action, exec, but you would not edit an existing line in the rebase instructions to use it as with the other actions, since it does not say to do anything with a commit; rather, the rest of the line is a just shell command for Git to run. A typical use for this is to test the preceding commit in some way, to make sure you haven't accidentally broken the content; you might add `exec make test`, for example, to run an automated software test. Git will stop if an exec command exits with a nonzero status. You can also give a single command with the `git rebase --exec` option, which will be run after every commit; this is a shortcut for inserting that same exec line after every commit in the sequencer directions.

## CHAPTER 5

Branching

Now that you know how to create a repository and commit to a single branch, it's time to learn about using multiple branches. Branches allow different versions of the same content to evolve independently at the same time, while you periodically recombine the contributions from different branches in a process called "merging." When you switch from one branch to another, Git updates your working tree to reflect the state of the repository content in the tip commit of the new branch.

A typical use for a branch is to work on a new software feature in isolation, without adding it to the main line of development of the project; these are often called "feature" or "topic" branches. You work on the feature branch while developing that feature, and switch to the *master* branch to work on the main project (which does not yet contain the new feature code). Periodically, you merge *master* into your feature branch, so you're working on up-to-date code and notice and resolve any conflicts. When the feature is ready, you do the opposite: merge the feature branch into *master*, adding the new code to the main version of the project.

Another use for multiple branches is to continue maintenance on older versions of software. When you release version 1.0 of your product, it gets its own branch. Product development continues, but you may need to apply bug fixes or new features to that version even after you've released 2.0, for customers who are still using the older version; the 1.0 branch allows you to do that (and `git cherry-pick` is particularly useful in this case; see "git cherry-pick" on page 181).

The man page *gitworkflows(7)* presents several branching disciplines that may be directly useful, or give you ideas on how to structure your own projects in other ways. Some of these are used in the development of Git itself.

The Default Branch, master

A new Git repository created with `git init` has a single branch with the default name *master*. There is nothing special about this name aside from being used as a default, and you can rename or delete it if you like. The *master* branch is conventionally used if there is only one branch in a repository, or if there are several but there is a single, clear main line of development.

If you try to use the *master* branch in a brand-new repository, however, you'll get perhaps unexpected results; for example:

```
$ git init
Initialized empty Git repository in /u/res/zork/.git/
$ git log
fatal: bad default revision 'HEAD'
```

Git could be more helpful here, since getting a "fatal" error with a newly created repository strongly suggests that something is broken. The error message is technically correct, though. Git has initialized the HEAD ref to point to *master*, making *master* the current branch. However, a branch name is just a ref pointing to the latest commit on the branch—and there are no commits yet in this new, empty repository, and so there is no *master* branch ref yet. When you make your first commit, Git will create the *master* branch with it.

Making a New Branch

The usual way to make a new branch named *alvin* is:

```
$ git checkout -b alvin
Switched to a new branch 'alvin'
```

This creates the branch *alvin* pointing at the current commit, and switches to it. Any existing changes to the index or working tree are preserved and will now be committed to *alvin* rather than to the previous branch (which is still there). Until one branch progresses, both branches point to the same commit. Until both progress independently, one branch still points to an earlier commit on the other. See Figure 5-1.

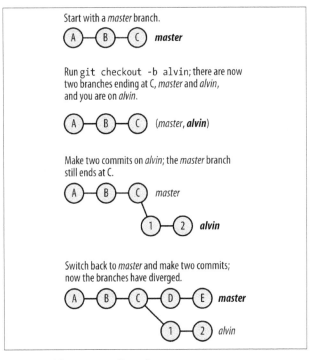

Figure 5-1. The progress of branch names

You can also specify a commit at which to start the new branch, rather than the current one, for example:

```
$ git checkout -b simon 9c6a1fad
Switched to a new branch 'simon'
```

This starts a new branch at the named commit and switches to it. If you have conflicting uncommitted changes, though, you will have to deal with them first. If you want to create the new branch but not switch to it, use `git branch simon` instead.

Switching Branches

The usual tool for switching branches is `git checkout`, of which the `-b` option given previously is just a special case: switching to a branch that doesn't yet exist is creating a new branch.

The only thing that *has* to happen to switch branches is to change the HEAD symbolic ref to point to the new branch name. The HEAD by definition indicates the branch that you are "on," and switching to a branch means that you are then "on" that branch. Here, `git symbolic-ref HEAD` shows the ref (branch name) to which HEAD points:

```
$ git symbolic-ref HEAD
refs/heads/theodore
$ git checkout simon
Switched to branch 'simon'
$ git symbolic-ref HEAD
refs/heads/simon
```

Technically, you could update the HEAD ref directly with `git update-ref`, but this isn't usually done and would be very confusing by itself; normally, you want your working tree and index to match the new branch tip when you switch branches, taking into account any uncommitted changes you may have. `git checkout` does all of these things, and more. Suppose you have two branches named *master* and *commander*, and you're currently on *master*. To switch to *commander*, simply use:

```
$ git checkout commander
Switched to branch 'commander'
```

This attempts to do three things:

1. Change the HEAD symref to point to the *commander* branch

2. Reset the index to match the tip of the new branch

3. Update the working tree to match the index (this is called "checking out" the index, which gives the command its name)

If these succeed, then you are now on the *commander* branch, with an index and working tree that match the tip of that branch. The following are some possible complications.

Uncommitted Changes

Suppose you have uncommitted changes to a tracked file when you try to switch branches. There are now four versions of the file in play: the two in the tip commits of the *master* and *commander* branches, and the two in your working tree and index (one or both of which have been altered, depending on whether you have staged the changes with git add). If the committed versions in the current and destination branches are the same, then Git will preserve your altered versions when switching branches, since they represent the same sets of changes in the new branch as in the old. It reminds you of a modified file *foo* thus:

```
$ git checkout commander
M       foo
Switched to branch 'commander'
```

If the committed versions differ, however, or if the file does not exist at all in the destination branch, then Git warns you and refuses to switch:

```
$ git checkout commander
error: Your local changes to the following files would
be overwritten by checkout:
        foo
Please, commit your changes or stash them before you
can switch branches. Aborting
```

stash refers to the `git stash` command, which lets you conveniently save and restore uncommitted changes; see "git stash" on page 188.

Check Out with Merge

`git checkout` has a `--merge` (`-m`) option to help with this case. It performs a three-way merge between your working tree and the new branch, with the current branch as the base; it leaves you on the new branch, with the merge result in the working tree. As with any merge, you may have conflicts to resolve; see "Merge Conflicts" on page 98.

Untracked Files

Git ignores untracked files while switching branches, unless the file exists in the target branch; then it aborts, even if the versions in the working tree and destination branch are the same. You can use the `--merge` option to get around this without having to delete the untracked file, only to have Git restore it a moment later. The merge operation results in the same file, in this case.

Losing Your Head

If you directly check out a specific commit rather than a branch, say with a command like `git checkout 520919b0`, then Git gives the odd and rather dire-sounding warning that you are now in "detached HEAD state." Fear not, Ichabod; all will be well. "Detached HEAD" simply means that the HEAD ref now points directly at a commit rather than referring to a particular branch by name. Git operates normally in this mode: you can make commits, and the HEAD ref moves forward as usual. The important thing to remember is that there is no branch tracking this work, so if you switch back to a branch with `git checkout branch`, you will simply discard any commits you've made while in detached HEAD mode: the HEAD ref then points to the branch you're on, and no ref remains marking the commit you left. Git warns you about this too, along with the commit ID you just left so that you can go back to it if you want. You can give your anonymous branch a name at any time while you're in detached HEAD mode, with `git checkout -b` *name.*

Deleting a Branch

When you ask Git to delete a branch, it simply deletes a pointer: a branch name ref that points to the branch tip. It does not delete the content of the branch, that is, remove from the object database all commits reachable from the pointer; it couldn't necessarily do that safely even if that were desired, since some of those commits might be part of other branches. To delete the branch *simon*, then:

```
$ git branch -d simon
Deleted branch simon (was 6273a3b0).
```

It may not be so simple, though; you might see this instead:

```
$ git branch -d simon
error: The branch 'simon' is not fully merged.
If you are sure you want to delete it, run
'git branch -D simon'.
```

Git is warning that you might lose history by deleting this branch. Even though it would not actually delete any commits right away, some or all of the commits on the branch would become unreachable if they are not part of some other branch as well. You could undo this mistake easily if you noticed it right away, as Git names the commit ID of the branch ref it removes, and it might be in a reflog as well; you could use `git checkout -b simon 6273a3b0` to restore the branch. It would get harder if you didn't notice until later, though, and perhaps impossible if that were after garbage collection had actually deleted the commits in question, and no one else had a copy of them.

For the branch *simon* to be "fully merged" into another branch, its tip commit must be an ancestor of the other branch's tip, making the commits in *simon* a subset of the other branch. This makes it safe to delete *simon*, since all its commits will remain part of the repository history via the other branch. It must be "fully" merged, because it may have been merged several times already, but now have commits added since the last merge that are not contained in the other branch.

Git doesn't check every other branch in the repository, though; just two:

1. The current branch (HEAD)

2. The upstream branch, if there is one

The "upstream branch" for *simon* would usually be *origin/simon*, referring to a branch in the repository from which this one was cloned, and with which this local *simon* branch coordinates via the push/pull mechanism. You can list upstream branches with `git branch -vv`; the upstream for each branch, if any, is listed in square brackets on the right:

```
$ git branch -vv
* master 8dd6fdc0 [origin/master: ahead 6] find acorns
  simon  6273a3b0 [origin/simon]: sing shrilly
```

If *simon* is fully merged in the current branch, then Git deletes it with no complaint. If it is not, but it is fully merged in its upstream branch, then Git proceeds with a warning:

```
$ git branch -d simon
warning: deleting branch 'simon' that has been merged
to 'refs/remotes/origin/simon', but not yet merged to
HEAD.
Deleted branch simon (was 6273a3b0).
```

Being fully merged in its upstream indicates that the commits in *simon* have been pushed to the origin repository, so that even if you lose them here, they may at least be saved elsewhere.

In Figure 5-2, *simon* has been merged into *master* before, but it and *master* have diverged since commit 2, and so *simon* is not now "fully merged" into *master*. It is fully merged into the upstream branch *origin/master*, however.

Since Git doesn't check other branches, it may be safe to delete a branch because you know it is fully merged into another one; you can do this with the -D option as indicated, or switch to that branch first and let Git confirm the fully merged status for you.

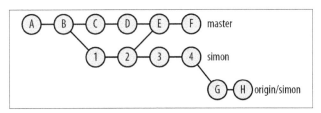

Figure 5-2. "merged" and "fully merged"

Deleting the branch from the origin repository is not so obvious:

```
$ git push origin :simon
```

This is the general syntax for directly updating a remote ref. In this case, the local object name to the left of the colon is blank, meaning to just delete the remote ref.

WHEN TO DELETE A BRANCH?

You most commonly delete a branch when it is private to you—that is, you created it in your own repository and have never pushed it elsewhere, and you have no further use for it. You can delete a branch from an upstream repository as just shown (assuming you're allowed to), but the effect of that does not automatically spread to other people coordinating through that repository. Their git pull will not delete their corresponding remote-tracking branch (they would need to use git fetch --prune for that), and any corresponding local downstream branches they've created in their own repositories will not be affected in any case. The general principle at work here is that a branch indicates a set of commits that are of interest; once a branch exists in your repository, it's up to you to decide whether you're no longer interested. Another person's action should not unilaterally make that decision for you.

Renaming a Branch

Renaming a local branch is simple:

```
$ git branch -m old new
```

There is no direct way to rename the corresponding branch in a remote repository, however; you must separately push the new branch and delete the old one:

```
$ git push -u origin new
$ git push origin :old
```

You will need to tell others that you've done this, since when they pull they will get the new branch, but they will have to manually delete the old name with `git branch -d`. "Renaming" a branch is not actually a Git operation per se; `git branch -m` is just a shortcut for the create/delete routine.

## CHAPTER 6

Tracking Other Repositories

This chapter discusses copying or "cloning" an existing repository, and thereafter sharing changes between original and clone using the Git "push" and "pull" commands.

Cloning a Repository

The `git clone` command initializes a new repository with the contents of another one and sets up tracking branches in the new repository so that you can easily coordinate changes between the two with the push/pull mechanism. We call the first repository a "remote" (even if it is in fact on the same host), and by default, this remote is named *origin*; you can change this with the `--origin` (`-o`) option, or with `git remote rename` later on. You can view and manipulate remotes with `git remote`; a repository can have more than one remote with which it synchronizes different sets of branches.

After cloning the remote repository, Git checks out the remote HEAD branch (often *master*); you can have it check out a different branch with `-b branch`, or none at all with `-n`:

```
$ git clone http://nifty-software.org/foo.git
Cloning into 'foo'...
remote: Counting objects: 528, done.
remote: Compressing objects: 100% (425/425), done.
remote: Total 528 (delta 100), reused 528 (delta 100)
```

```
Receiving objects: 100% (528/528), 1.31 MiB | 1.30 Mi…
Resolving deltas: 100% (100/100), done.
```

If you give a second argument, Git will create a directory with that name for the new repository (or use an existing directory, so long as it's empty); otherwise, it derives the name from that of source repository using some ad hoc rules. For example, *foo* stays *foo*, but *foo.git* and *bar/foo* also become *foo*.

You can specify the remote repository with a URL as shown, or with a simple path to a directory in the filesystem containing a Git repository. Git supports a number of transport schemes natively to access remote repositories, including HTTP, HTTPS, its own *git* protocol, FTP, FTPS, and rsync.

Git will also automatically use SSH if you use the *ssh* URL scheme (*ssh://*), or give the repository as [user@]host:/path/to/repo; this uses SSH to run git upload-pack on the remote side. If the path is relative (no leading slash), then it is usually relative to the home directory of the login account on the server, though this depends on the SSH server configuration. You can specify the SSH program to use with the environment variable GIT_SSH (the default is, unsurprisingly, ssh). With the long form you can also give a TCP port number for the server, e.g., ssh://nifty-software.org:2222/foo.

Clones and Hard Links

When you give the origin repository as a simple directory name, and the new repository is on the same filesystem, Git uses Unix "hard links" to the originals for certain files instead of copying them when populating the object database of the clone, saving time and disk space. This is safe for two reasons. First, the semantics of hard links are such that someone deleting a shared file in the origin repository has no effect on you; files remain accessible until the last link is removed. Second, because of content-based addressing, Git objects are immutable; an object with a given ID will not suddenly change out from under you. You can turn off this feature and force actual copying with --no-hardlinks, or by using a URL with the "file" scheme to access the same path: *file:///path/to/repo.git* (the empty hostname between the second and third slash indicates the local host).

NOTE

When we refer to a "local" repository in this section, we mean one accessible to Git using the filesystem, as opposed to needing an explicit network connection (SSH, HTTP, and so on). That may not in fact be "local" to the host itself, however (meaning on hardware directly attached to it); it could be on a file server accessed over the network via NFS or CIFS, for example. Thus, a repository that is "local" to Git might still be "remote" from the host.

Shared Clone

An even faster method when cloning a local repository is the `--shared` option. Rather than either copy or link files between the origin and clone repositories, this simply configures the clone to search the object database of the origin in addition to its own. Initially, the object database of the clone is completely empty, because all the objects it needs are in the origin. New objects you create in the clone are added to its own database; the clone never modifies the origin's database via this link.

It's important to keep in mind, though, that the clone is now dependent on the origin repository to function; if the origin is not accessible, Git may abort, complaining that its object database is corrupted because it can't find objects that used to be there. If you know you're going to remove the origin repository, you can use `git repack -a` in the clone to force it to copy all the objects it needs into its own database. If you have to recover from accidentally deleting the origin, you can edit *.git/objects/info/alternates* if you have another local copy. You can also add the other repository with `git remote add`, then use `git fetch --all remote` to pull over the objects you need.

Another issue with shared clones is garbage collection: if garbage collection is later run on the remote and by then it has removed some refs you still have, objects that are still part of your history may just disappear, again leading to "database corrupted" errors on your side.

Bare Repositories

A "bare" repository is one without a working tree or index, created by `git init --bare`; the files normally under *.git* are right inside the repository directory instead. A bare repository is usually a coordination point for a centralized workflow: each person pushes and pulls to and from the bare copy, which represents the current "official" state of the project. No one uses the bare copy directly, so it doesn't need a working tree (you can't push into a non-bare repository if the push tries to update the currently checked-out branch, as that would change the branch out from under the person using it). Another use for a bare repository, using `git clone --bare`, is shown in the next section.

Reference Repositories

Suppose that:

- You want to have checkouts of multiple branches of the same project at once; or

- Several people with access to the same filesystem want clones of the same repository; or

- Some process requires you to clone the same repository frequently

…and that the repository takes a long time to clone; perhaps it has a large history, or there's a slow network link in the way. A solution is to share one local copy of the object database, rather than pull it over repeatedly, but using `git clone --shared` is awkward for this, because it introduces two levels of push/pull: you push from your clone to the local shared (bare) clone, and then you have to push from there to the origin (and similarly for pull).

Git has another option that exactly fits this bill: a "reference repository." Here's how it works: first, we make a bare clone of the remote repository, to be shared locally as a reference repository (hence named "refrep"):

```
$ git clone --bare http://foo/bar.git refrep
Cloning into 'refrep'...
remote: Counting objects: 21259, done.
remote: Compressing objects: 100% (6730/6730), done.
Receiving objects: 100% (21259/21259), 39.84 MiB | 12…
remote: Total 21259 (delta 15427), reused 20088 (delt…
Resolving deltas: 100% (15427/15427), done.
```

Then, we clone the remote again, but this time giving *refrep* as a reference:

```
$ git clone --reference refrep http://foo/bar.git
Cloning into 'bar'...
done.
```

This happens very quickly, and you see no messages about transferring objects, because none were needed; all the objects were already available in the reference repository. Others using this repository in your site can use this command to create their clones as well, sharing the reference.

The key difference between this and the --shared option is that you are still tracking the remote repository, not the *refrep* clone. When you pull, you still contact *http://foo/*, but you don't need to wait for it to send any objects that are already stored locally in *refrep*; when you push, you are updating the branches and other refs of the *foo* repository directly.

Of course, as soon as you and others start pushing new commits, the reference repository will become out of date, and you'll start to lose some of the benefit. Periodically, you can run git fetch --all in *refrep* to pull in any new objects. A single reference repository can be a cache for the objects of any number of others; just add them as remotes in the reference:

```
$ git remote add zeus http://olympus/zeus.git
$ git fetch --all zeus
```

Local, Remote, and Tracking Branches

When you clone a repository, Git sets up "remote-tracking"
branches corresponding to the branches in the origin repository.
These are branches in your local repository, which show you the
state of the origin branches at the time of your last push or pull.

When you check out a branch that doesn't yet exist, but there is a remote-tracking branch by that name, Git automatically creates it and sets its upstream to be that tracking branch, so that subsequent push/pull operations will synchronize your local version of this branch with the remote's version. For example, when you first clone a repository, Git checks out the remote's HEAD branch, so this happens right away for one branch:

```
$ git clone git://nifty-software.org/nifty.git
...
$ cd nifty
$ git branch --all
master
origin/master
origin/topic
```

To begin with, your local and remote-tracking branches for *master* are at the same commit:

```
$ git log --oneline --decorate=short
3a9ee5f3 (origin/master, master) in principio
```

If you add a commit, you will see your branch pull ahead:

```
$ git log --oneline --decorate=short
3307465c (master) the final word
3a9ee5f3 (origin/master) in principio
```

If you run git fetch, you may find that someone else has also added a commit, and the branches have now diverged:

```
$ git log --graph --all
* commit baa699bc (origin/master)
| Author: Nefarious O. Committer <nefarious@qoxp.net>
| Date:   Fri Aug 24 09:33:10 2012 -0400
|
|     not quite
|
| * commit 3307465c (master)
|/  Author: Richard E. Silverman <res@qoxp.net>
|   Date:   Fri Aug 24 09:32:54 2012 -0400
|
|       the final word
|
* commit 3a9ee5f3
```

```
Author: Mysterious Author <ma@qoxp.net>
Date:   Fri Aug 24 09:42:27 2012 -0400

    in principio
```

`git pull` will try to merge the now-distinct branches, which is necessary before you can push your changes; otherwise, `git push` would update *origin/master* to match your *master*, and lose commit baa699bc in the process.

Synchronization: Push and Pull

Having cloned a repository, you use `git push` and `git pull` to reconcile your changes with those of others using the same upstream repository. Various things can happen when your changes conflict with theirs; we'll start discussing that here, and continue in Chapter 7.

Pulling

If a branch *foo* is tracking a branch in a remote repository, that remote is configured as `branch.foo.remote` in this repository, and is said to be the remote associated with this branch, or just the "remote of this branch." `git pull` updates the tracking branches of the remote for the current branch (or of the `origin` remote if the branch has none), fetching new objects as needed and recording new upstream branches. If the current branch is tracking an upstream in that remote, Git then tries to reconcile the current state of your branch with that of the newly updated tracking branch. If only you or the upstream has added commits to this branch since your last pull, then this will succeed with a "fast-forward" update: one branch head just moves forward along the branch to catch up with the other. If both sides have added commits, though, then a fast-forward update is not possible: just setting one side's branch head to match the other would discard the opposite side's new commits (they would become unreachable from the new head). This is the situation shown previously, and the solution is a merge:

```
$ git log --graph --oneline
*   2ee20b94    (master, origin/master) Merge branch…
|\
| * 3307465c    the final word
* | baa699bc    not quite
|/
* 3a9ee5f3      in principio
```

The merge commit 2ee20b94 brings together the divergent local and upstream versions of the branch, and allows both *master* and *origin/master* to advance to the same commit without losing information. git pull will automatically attempt this, and if it can combine the actual changes cleanly, this will all happen smoothly. If not, Git will stop and ask you to deal with the conflicts before making the merge commit; we'll discuss that process in Chapter 7.

Pushing

git push is the converse of git pull, with which you apply your changes to the upstream repository. If, as before, your history has diverged from that of the remote, Git will refuse to push unless you address the divergence, which you do by pulling first (as Git helpfully reminds you):

```
$ git push
To git://nifty-software.org/nifty.git
! [rejected]        master -> master (non-fast-forward)
error: failed to push some refs to 'git://nifty-softw…
hint: Updates were rejected because the tip of your
hint: current branch is behind its remote
hint: counterpart. Merge the remote changes
hint: (e.g. 'git pull') before pushing again.  See
hint: the 'Note about fast-forwards' in 'git push
hint: --help' for details.
```

Once you pull and resolve any conflicts, you can push again successfully. The goal of pulling with regard to pushing is to integrate the upstream changes with your own so that you can push without discarding any commits in the upstream history. You may accomplish that by merging as previously shown, or by "rebasing" (see "Pull with Rebase" on page 89).

If you have added a local branch of your own and want to start sharing it with others, use the `-u` option to have Git add your branch to the remote, and set up tracking for your local branch in the usual way, for example:

```
$ git push -u origin new-branch
```

After this initial setup you can use just `git push` on this branch, with no options or arguments, to push to the same remote.

Push Defaults

There are several approaches Git can use when given no specific remote and ref to push (just plain `git push`, as opposed to `git push remote branch`):

matching
>   Push all branches with matching local and remote names

upstream
>   Push the current branch to its upstream (making push and pull symmetric operations)

simple
>   Like upstream, but check that the branch names are the same (to guard against mistaken upstream settings)

current
>   Push the current branch to a remote one with the same name (creating it if necessary)

nothing
>   Push nothing (require explicit arguments)

You can set this with the `push.default` configuration variable. The default as of this writing is matching, but with Git 2.0, this will change to simple, which is more conservative and avoids easy accidental pushing of changes on other branches that are not yet ready to be published. To choose an option, think about what would happen in your particular situation if you accidentally typed `git push` with each of these options in force, and pick the one that makes you most comfortable. Remember that like all options, you can set this on a per-repository basis (see "Basic Configuration" on page 33).

Pull with Rebase

Along with the facility of merge commits comes the need to make them wisely. The notion of what a merge should indicate with respect to content is subjective and varies as a matter of version control discipline and style, but generally you want a merge to point out a substantive combination of two lines of development. Certainly, too many merges creates a commit graph that is difficult to read, thus reducing the usefulness of the structural merge feature itself. In this context, certain workflows can easily create what one might call "spurious merges," which do not actually correspond to such merging of content. Having lots of these clutters up the commit graph, and makes it difficult to discern the real history of a project.

As an example: suppose you and a colleague are coordinating your individual repositories via push/pull with a shared central one. You commit a change to your repository, while he commits an unrelated change on the same branch. The changes might be to different files, or even to the same file but such that they do not require manual conflict resolution. If he pushes first, then as described earlier, your subsequent push will fail, so you will pull; then Git will do a successful automatic merge (since the changes were independent), and this becomes part of the repository history with your final push. But if you think of a merge as a deliberate step to signal the combination of conflicting or substantially different content, then you don't really want this merge. The telltale sign of this sort of spurious merge is that it's purely an artifact of timing; if the order of events had instead been:

1. You commit and push.

2. He pulls.

3. He commits and pushes.

then there would have been no conflict, and no merge. This ob-
servation is the key to avoiding such merges using `git pull
--rebase`, which reorders your changes. "Rebasing" is a more
general idea, which we treat in "Rebasing" on page 149; the pull-
with-rebase option is a special case. Briefly, what happens is this:
suppose your *master* branch diverged from its upstream several
commits back. For each divergent commit on your branch, Git
constructs a patch representing the changes introduced by that
commit; then it applies these in order starting at the tip of the
upstream tracking branch *origin/master*. After applying each
patch, Git makes a new commit preserving the author information and message from the original commit. Finally, it resets your
master branch to point to the last of these commits. The effect is
to "replay" your work on top of the upstream branch as new
commits, rather than affecting a merge with your existing .commits.

In the earlier example, `git pull --rebase` would produce the
following simple, linear history instead of the "merge bubble"
previously pictured, with its extra commit:

```
* 1e6f2cb2      the final word
* baa699bc      not quite
* 3a9ee5f3      in principio
```

A push now will succeed without further work (and without
merging), because you've simply added to the upstream branch;
it will be a fast-forward update of that branch. Note that the
commit ID for "the final word" has changed; that's because it's a
new commit made by replaying the changes of the original on
top of commit baa699bc.

If `git pull` starts a merge when you know there's no need for it,
you can always cancel it by giving an empty commit message, or
with `git merge --abort` if the merge failed leaving you in
conflict-resolution mode. If you complete such a merge and want
to undo it, use `git reset HEAD^` to move your branch back again,
discarding the merge commit. You can then use `git pull
--rebase` instead. You can set a specific branch to automatically
use `--rebase` when pulling:

```
$ git config branch.branch-name.rebase yes
```

and the configuration variable `branch.autosetuprebase` controls
how this is set for new branches:

`never`
> Default: do not set rebase

`remote`
> Set for branches tracking remote branches

`local`
> Set for branches tracking other branches in the same
> repository

`always`
> Set for all tracking branches

Notes

1. If you know it's the right thing to do, you can perform
    destructive, non–fast-forward updates with the `--force`
    option to either push or pull, although in the case of push
    the remote must be configured to allow it; repositories cre-
    ated with `git init --shared` have this disabled by setting
    `receive.denyNonFastForwards`.

    Beware! It's one thing to do a forced pull; you're just dis-
    carding some of your own history. A forced push, on the
    other hand, causes grief for other people, who will be un-
    able to pull cleanly as a result. For a repository shared by a
    small set of people in close communication, or that is a
    read-only reference for most, this may be occasionally ap-
    propriate. For anything shared by a wide audience, though,
    you really don't want to do this.

2. The command `git remote show remote` gives a useful
    summary of the status of your repository in relation to a
    remote:

    ```
    $ git remote show origin
    * remote origin
    ```

```
Fetch URL: git://tamias.org/chipmunks.git
Push  URL: git://tamias.org/chipmunks.git
HEAD branch: master
Remote branches:
  alvin     tracked
  theodore tracked
  simon     tracked
Local branches configured for 'git pull':
  alvin  merges with remote alvin
  simon  merges with remote simon
Local refs configured for 'git push':
  alvin  pushes to alvin  (up to date)
  simon  pushes to simon  (local out of date)
```

Note that unlike most informational commands, this actually examines the remote repository, so it will run *ssh* or otherwise use the network if necessary. You can use the -n switch to avoid this; Git will skip those operations that require contacting the remote and note them as such in the output.

3. `git branch -vv` gives a more compact summary without contacting the remote (and thus reflects the state as of the last fetch or pull; remember that the remote might have changed in the meantime). The following shows a purely local *master* branch, plus two branches tracking remote ones: *alvin* is up to date with respect to its upstream, whereas the current local branch, *simon*, has moved three commits forward:

   ```
   $ git branch -vv
     alvin  7e55cfe3 [origin/alvin] I love chestnuts.
     master a675f734 Chipmunks are the real nuts.
   * simon  9b0e3dc5 [origin/simon: ahead 3] Walnuts!
   ```

   (This state is not one resulting from previous examples.)

4. There appears to be a lot of pointless redundancy in many of these messages; things like "*alvin* pushes to *alvin*," or updates indicating "*master→master*." The reason is that the default, common situation is for corresponding local and remote branches to have matching names, but this need not be the case; for more complex situations, you can have

arbitrary associations, and the Git messages take this into account. For example, if you have a repository with two remotes each having a *master* branch, your local tracking branches can't both be named *master* as well. You could proceed this way:

```
$ git remote add foo git://foo.com/foo.git
$ git remote add bar http://bar.com/bar.git
$ git fetch --all
Fetching foo
remote: Counting objects: 6, done.
remote: Compressing objects: 100% (2/2), done.
remote: Total 6 (delta 0), reused 0 (delta 0)
Unpacking objects: 100% (6/6), done.
From foo git://foo.com/foo.git
 * [new branch]      master     -> foo/master
Fetching bar
remote: Counting objects: 5, done.
remote: Total 3 (delta 0), reused 0 (delta 0)
Unpacking objects: 100% (3/3), done.
From http://bar.com/bar.git
 * [new branch]      master     -> bar/master
$ git checkout -b foo-master --track foo/master
Branch foo-master set up to track remote branch
master from foo.
Switched to a new branch 'foo-master'
$ git checkout -b bar-master --track bar/master
Branch bar-master set up to track remote branch
master from bar.
Switched to a new branch 'bar-master'
$ git branch -vv
* bar-master f1ace62e [bar/master] bars are boring
  foo-master 11e4af82 [foo/master] foosball is fab
...
```

These messages from git clone:

```
 * [new branch]      master     -> foo/master
...
 * [new branch]      master     -> bar/master
...
```

might be a little confusing; they indicate that the remote branch *master* in each repository is now being tracked by local branches *foo/master* and *bar/master*, respectively (not that it somehow overwrote a local *master* branch, which might or might not exist and is not relevant here).

Access Control

In a word (or three): there is none.

It is important to understand that Git by itself does not provide any sort of authentication or comprehensive access control when accessing a remote repository. Git has no internal notion of "user" or "account," and although some specific actions may be forbidden by configuration (e.g., non–fast-forward updates), generally you can do whatever is possible with the operating-system level access controls in place. For example, remote repositories are often accessed via SSH. This usually means that you need to be able to log into an account on the remote machine (which account may be shared with other people); you can clone and pull from the repository if that account has read access to the repository files on that machine, and you can push to the repository if that account has write access. If you're using HTTP for access instead, then similar comments apply to the configuration of the web server and the account under which it accesses the repository. That's it. There is no way within Git to limit access to particular users according to more fine-grained notions, such as granting read-only access to one branch, commit access to another, and no access to a third. There are, however, third-party tools that add such features; Gitolite, Gitorious, and Gitosis are popular ones.

## CHAPTER 7

Merging

Merging is the process of combining the recent changes from several branches into a single new commit that is on all those branches. Most often there are only two branches involved, but in fact, there can be any number; if there are more than two, it is called an "octopus merge." When there are only two branches, the current branch is called "our" side of the merge, while the other branch is called "their" side. Since the octopus merge is unusual, we will generally assume a two-branch merge in this discussion.

We described how Git may start a merge for you as part of `git pull` (see "Pulling" on page 86), but you can also perform merges explicitly. Here's a typical scenario: you're working on a software project, and you have an idea for a new feature, but you don't want your experimental work on that feature to disturb your main development. So you create a branch named *feature* to contain the work:

```
$ git checkout -b feature
Switched to a new branch 'feature'
(explore brilliant idea...)
```

When you need to go back to work on the main part of your project, you commit your work on the *feature* branch and switch back to *master* (or whichever branch you need to work on):

```
$ git commit -am "must save brilliant thoughts"
[feature c6dbf36e]
 0 files changed
 create mode 100644 effulgent.c
 create mode 100644 epiphany.h
$ git checkout master
Switched to branch 'master'
(perform mundane chores...)
```

You continue like this for some time. Eventually, if you decide you don't like your feature idea, you can discard the work by deleting the branch with git branch -D feature. If you decide to keep it, however, at some point you'll want to incorporate it into the main project code, and you do this with a merge:

```
$ git checkout master
Switched to branch 'master'
$ git merge feature
Auto-merging main.c
Merge made by the 'recursive' strategy.
 effulgent.c | 452 +++++++++++++++++++++++++++
 epiphany.h  |  45 ++++++++++
 main.c      |  18 ++--
 3 files changed, 507 insertions(+), 9 deletion(-)
 create mode 100644 effulgent.c
 create mode 100644 epiphany.h
```

WARNING

It's best to have all your work committed before running git merge; that is, git status should show no outstanding changes or untracked files. Backing out of a merge to your initial state may prove difficult otherwise. You can use git stash as a quick way to save working changes and restore them later (see "git stash" on page 188).

This merge was simple. You had added the files *effulgent.c* and *epiphany.h* on the *feature* branch, and they did not exist on *master*, so Git just added them. You had made minor changes to *main.c* on both branches, but those changes did not conflict, so

Git combined them automatically and committed its merged version. The ASCII graph with filenames on the left is called a "diffstat"; it is a summary of the changes made by this commit. The lines of plus and minus signs represent the relative number of line additions ("insertions") and deletions made in the corresponding file.

Both aspects of merging have occurred here: content and structure. First, Git combined the content of both branches by adding and merging changes to files; then, it recorded the fact of the merge structurally by creating a merge commit tying both branches together in the commit graph. This indicates in the history those commits whose contents were combined to produce the new one, by making them its parents. A "merge commit" is defined simply as a commit having more than one parent.

You can continue this process as long as you like, working on the *feature* branch separately and periodically merging its work into *master*. If you do, you will probably also need to merge the other way as well, updating the *feature* branch with the latest work on *master*, so that you're not working on outdated code; for this, just do the reverse: switch to *feature* and run `git merge master`.

When your new feature is fully incorporated into the main development, and you no longer need to work on it separately, you can delete the *feature* branch with `git branch -d feature`; as discussed in "Deleting a Branch" on page 75, Git will complain if you haven't fully merged *feature* into *master*, to prevent you from accidentally losing work. Deleting *feature* doesn't delete any of its content or history; it just removes the name "feature" as a reference point, a place at which you intend to add independent commits later on—since you no longer need it. You can reuse "feature" as a branch name in the future if you want, and there will be no collision with the earlier usage; in fact, aside from possibly in commit messages or reflogs, once you delete a branch, there is no record in the repository proper that it ever existed! Branch names serve to indicate what parts of the object database are still of interest, and where development is still occurring; if a branch's content is merged into other branches, and you no longer need a line of development with that name, then you can just delete it, and reuse the name later for something else if you like. Similarly, looking back in the commit graph, it is not possible to know on which branch name a particular commit was made; even in a linear history, the current branch name might have been changed at some point in the past. It might be interesting or useful to know this in some situations, but Git just doesn't keep this information. Git branches are ephemeral in a sense, just tools for building the commit graph, which is what matters.

Merge Conflicts

The previous merge went smoothly, but what if you had made changes in the two branches that Git could not combine on its own? These are called "merge conflicts," and Git would stop and ask you to resolve them before committing. This process can range from simple to very complex, depending on the content and changes involved; fortunately, there are tools available to help, both in Git itself and with which Git can work. Let's walk through a simple example. Suppose you have a file *moebius* with the following contents:

```
hello
doctor
name
continue
yesterday
tomorrow
```

and you make commits on branches *chandra* and *floyd* changing it thus:

chandra	floyd
hello	hello
doctor	doctor
Jupiter	Europa
dolphin	monoliths
yesterday	yesterday
tomorrow	tomorrow

You have changed the same two lines on each side in different
ways, and Git's line-oriented merge approach will not attempt to
guess at your intent or combine the lines (e.g., form a single line
dolphin monoliths, interesting as those might be); it will signal
a merge conflict:

```
$ git checkout chandra
Switched to branch 'chandra'
$ git merge floyd
Auto-merging moebius
CONFLICT (content): Merge conflict in moebius
Automatic merge failed; fix conflicts and then commit
the result.
```

The phrase CONFLICT (content) indicates that the conflict is due
to irreconcilable content changes in this file. Git might indicate
other reasons as well, such as an add/add conflict, in which the
same filename is added to both branches but with different
contents.

TIP

If you start a merge and then want to cancel it—perhaps you
weren't expecting so many conflicts and you don't have time
to deal with them now—just use git merge --abort.

To get an overview of the merge state, use git status. Any
changes Git resolved on its own will be shown as already staged

for commit, and there is a separate section at the end for merge conflicts:

```
$ git status
...
# Unmerged paths:
#   (use "git add <file>..." to mark resolution)
#
#       both modified:      moebius
```

"Unmerged paths" are files with conflicts Git could not resolve. To find out what went wrong in detail, use git diff. This command not only shows the differences between various combinations of working tree, index, and commits; it also has a special mode for helping with merge conflicts:

```
$ git diff
diff --cc moebius
index 1fcbe134,08dbe186..00000000
--- a/moebius
+++ b/moebius
@@@ -1,6 -1,6 +1,11 @@@
  hello
  doctor
++<<<<<<< ours
 +Jupiter
 +dolphin
++=======
+ Europa
+ monoliths
++>>>>>>> theirs
  yesterday
  tomorrow
```

This display shows the alternative versions of the section in conflict, separated by ======= and marked with the corresponding branch: ours (the current branch) and theirs (in this case *floyd*, the branch we are merging into ours). As usual, git diff shows differences between the working tree and the index, which in this case are the conflicts yet to be resolved; changes already made and staged are not shown. You can use git diff --staged to see those; add --stat for an overview. You'll find that Git has updated the working file with similar markup:

```
hello
doctor
<<<<<<< ours
Jupiter
dolphin
=======
Europa
monoliths
>>>>>>> theirs
yesterday
tomorrow
```

Once you've edited the file to resolve the conflict, use `git add` to stage your fixed version for commit and remove it from the list of conflicted paths (if the resolution is actually to delete the file, use `git rm`). Once you've addressed all the conflicts and `git sta tus` no longer reports any unmerged paths, you can use `git com mit` to complete the merge. Git will present a commit message containing details about this merge including its branches and conflicts, which you can edit as you see fit; in this case:

```
Merge branch 'floyd' into chandra

Conflicts:
        moebius
```

and you can see you've created a "merge commit" having more than one parent:

```
$ git log --graph --oneline --decorate
*   aeba9d85  (HEAD, chandra) Merge branch 'floyd' in…
|\
| * a5374035  (floyd) back in black
* | e355785d  thanks for all the fish!
|/
* 50769fc9  star child
```

The other branch, *floyd*, has stayed where it was, while the current branch, *chandra*, has advanced one commit from e355785d to aeba9d85, and that last commit unifies the two branches. A new commit on *floyd* will cause them to diverge again, and you can merge again in the future if you need to (in either direction). Note that at this point, a simple `git log` will show commits from *both* branches, not just those made while on *chandra*:

```
$ git log --oneline --decorate
aeba9d85 (HEAD, chandra) Merge branch 'floyd' into ch…
a5374035 (floyd) back in black
e355785d thanks for all the fish!
50769fc9 star child
```

You might have expected to see only commits aeba9d85, e355785d, and 50769fc9. This presentation may seem odd at first, but it's just a different way of looking at the notion of "branch." A Git branch is defined as the set of all commits reachable in the commit graph from the branch tip; think of it as all commits that contributed content to the tip commit (which, after a merge, includes all commits prior to that one on both branches).

TIP

In simple cases, you may get what you think of as the history of "this branch" with `git log --first-parent`, which just follows the first parent of merge commits rather than all of them. However, this isn't guaranteed, and in more complex histories it won't mean much. Since Git allows nonlinear history, a simple list of commits is often not very useful, and you need visualization tools to help you interpret it (see "Visual Tools" on page 197).

Resolving Merge Conflicts

Git doesn't have built-in tools to interactively address merge conflicts directly; that's what external merge tools are for, which we'll consider shortly in "Merge Tools" on page 107. However, here are some tips for use in simple cases.

1. `git log -p --merge` shows all commits containing changes relevant to any unmerged files, on either branch, together with their diffs. This can help you identify the changes in the history that led to the conflicts.

2. If you want to discard all the changes from one side of the merge, use `git checkout --{ours,theirs}` *file* to update the working file with the copy from the current or other branch, followed by `git add` *file* to stage the change and mark the conflict as resolved.

3. Having done that, if you would like to apply *some* of the changes from the opposite side, use `git checkout -p` *branch file*. This starts an interactive loop that allows you to selectively apply or edit differing sections (see the "patch" item in the "Interactive Mode" section of *git-add(1)* for details).

In our example, if you decided to keep your version as a default, but selectively apply changes from the other branch, you could do:

```
$ git checkout --ours moebius
$ git add moebius
$ git checkout -p floyd moebius
diff --git b/moebius a/moebius
index 1fcbe134..08dbe186 100644
--- b/moebius
+++ a/moebius
@@ -1,6 +1,6 @@
hello
doctor
-Jupiter
-dolphin
+Europa
+monoliths
yesterday
tomorrow
Apply this hunk to index and worktree [y,n,q,a,d,/,e,…
y - apply this hunk to index and worktree
n - do not apply this hunk to index and worktree
q - quit; do not apply this hunk nor any of the remai…
a - apply this hunk and all later hunks in the file
...
$ git add moebius
```

Notes

1. If the current branch is already contained in the other (that is, HEAD is an ancestor of the other branch tip), then `git merge` will just move the current branch up to meet the other in a "fast-forward" update, and not make a new commit at all. You can force a merge commit anyway with `git merge --no-ff` ("no fast-forward"), if you have some reason to do so.

2. If the converse is true, and the other branch is already contained in this one, then Git will simply say that the current branch is "already up-to-date," and do nothing. The goal of the merge is to incorporate into the current branch any changes on the other branch since the two diverged—but they haven't diverged.

3. If you want to use Git's content-merging and conflict-resolution machinery, but do not want to create a merge commit, use `git merge --squash`. This operates like a normal merge with regard to content, but the commit it creates is just on the current branch (that is, has a single parent and does not connect to the other branch in the commit graph).

4. You can use `git merge -m` to specify a commit message just as with `git commit`, although remember that Git provides useful information in its supplied message, which you may prefer to start with and edit instead (which happens by default).

5. Use `git merge --no-commit` to stop Git from committing when an automatic merge succeeds, in case you want to have a look first. This isn't strictly necessary, since you could always abort the commit by giving a blank commit message, or make any changes you want afterward and use `git commit --amend`.

6. Git records that a merge is in progress by setting the ref `MERGE_HEAD` to point to the other branch; this is how it knows to make a merge commit (as opposed to a simple

commit on the current branch) even when there are intervening commands while you resolve conflicts.

Details on Merging

When merging, Git considers the changes that have occurred on
the branches in question since they last diverged. In the previous
example, the branches *chandra* and *floyd* last diverged at commit
50769fc9, so the changes to be reconciled were those in commits
e355785d and a5374035. These branches might have diverged
and been merged several times previously, but you will only be
asked to deal with new changes since that last happened. Some
other version control systems do not have this feature, so that
merging branches repeatedly is a problem: you end up resolving
the same conflicts over and over.

More precisely, when merging several branches, Git seeks a
"merge base": a recent common ancestor of all the branch tips,
to use as a reference point for arbitrating changes. Although in
complicated situations there might be multiple possibilities for a
merge base (see *git-merge-base(1)*), in the common case of our
example, there is a single obvious choice, which Git finds automatically. Since our merge now involves three commits—two
branch tips and the merge base—it is called a "three-way merge."

Recall that `git status` showed our conflicts, the "unmerged
paths." Where does it keep this information? There are conflict
markers in the working files, but it would be slow to read all the
files for this purpose, and in any case that wouldn't help for a
modify/delete conflict. The answer demonstrates yet again the
usefulness of the index. When there is a merge conflict for a file,
Git simply stores not one version of the file in the index, but three:
those belonging to the merge base and to the current and "other"
branches, numbered 1, 2, and 3, respectively. The number is
called the "stage" of the file and is a distinct property of an index
entry along with the filename, mode bits, and so on. In fact, there
is a third stage, 0, which is the usual state of an entry that has no

associated merge conflict. We can see this using `git ls-files`, which shows the contents of the index. Prior to the merge, we see:

```
$ git ls-files -s --abbrev
100644 1fcbe134 0       moebius
```

The fields here are the mode bits, ID of the blob object holding the file's contents, the stage number, and the filename. After running `git merge floyd` and getting a conflict for this file, we see something very different (using `-u` instead of `-s` would show only unmerged paths; here we have only one file anyway):

```
$ git ls-files -s --abbrev
100644 30b7cdab 1       moebius
100644 1fcbe134 2       moebius
100644 08dbe186 3       moebius
```

Note that the ID of stage 2 matches what was previously stage 0 earlier, since stage 2 is the version on the current branch. You can use `git cat-file` to see the contents of the different stages, here the stage 1 merge-base version:

```
$ git cat-file -p 30b7cdab
hello
doctor
name
continue
yesterday
tomorrow
```

You can refer to a specific stage of a file with the syntax `:n:path`; so `git show :1:moebius` is an easier equivalent for this.

Git records the three commits into the index in this way at the start of the merge. It then follows a set of simple rules to quickly resolve the easy cases; for example:

- If all three stages match, reduce to a single stage 0.

- If stage 1 matches stage 2, then reduce to a single stage 0 matching stage 3 (or vice versa): one side made a change while the other did nothing.

- If stage 1 matches stage 2, but there is no stage 3, then remove the file: we made no change, while the other branch deleted it, so accept the other branch's deletion.

- If stages 1 and 2 differ, and there is no stage 3, then report a "modify/delete" conflict: we changed the file, while the other branch deleted it; the user must decide what to do.

…and so forth. Note that for matching, Git doesn't need to fetch the actual files; it can just compare the blob object IDs already in the index, since they are hashes of the files' contents. This is very fast; content-based addressing wins again. You can read about this process in more detail in *git-read-tree(1)*. Any files that can't be easily resolved this way must then actually be examined to attempt merging their contents.

Merge Tools

Merging can be a complex job, with you staring at scores of conflicting sections of source code changes from yourself and other people, and trying to combine them into a single working whole. There are tools available that go far beyond the simple text output of `git diff` in helping you to visualize and resolve such conflicts. Git integrates smoothly with these external "merge tools," to help you get the job done more easily. Git supports over a dozen free and commercial merge tools out of the box, including *araxis, emerge, opendiff, kdiff3,* and *gvimdiff.* It also defines an interface with which you can use most any such tool, usually requiring only a simple wrapper script to connect it to Git.

We can't delve into the details of the individual merge tools; many of them are complex programs in their own right and would require another small book each to describe. Here, we'll just describe how they work with Git generally.

The driver for using a merge tool is `git mergetool`. Once invoked, this command runs over all the files with merge conflicts, asking for each if you want to invoke the selected merge tool on the file. The default merge tool is *opendiff,* but you can set a different default with the `merge.tool` Git configuration variable. The tool will usually present you with a view of the "ours" and "theirs" versions of the file, along with the merge base, and provide ways to move from one change or conflict to the next, select which side's change to use (or combine them), etc. When you quit the merge tool indicating success, Git will add your merged version to the index (thus marking this conflict as resolved), and go on to the next unmerged file.

Notes

- The `-y` switch to `git mergetool` tells it to run the tool on all unmerged files, without pausing to prompt yes or no for each one.

- `git mergetool` leaves a backup *foo.orig* for each file *foo* it processes, since you might have modified it yourself before running the merge tool. You can set `mergetool.keepBackup` no to turn off this feature. Actually, Git still makes the backup; it just deletes it when the merge tool exits successfully, so that the backup is still there in case the tool were to crash.

- If a merge tool exits unexpectedly or doesn't work properly, you may see files like these left behind (for the file *main.c*):

  ```
  main.c.BACKUP.62981.c
  main.c.BASE.62981.c
  main.c.LOCAL.62981.c
  main.c.REMOTE.62981.c
  ```

  These are the temporary files that Git uses to pass the various file versions to the merge tool.

Custom Merge Tools

If you want to use a merge tool not directly supported by Git, it need only obey some simple conventions; usually, you'll write a glue script to accommodate them. Git passes four filenames to the tool as environment variables:

LOCAL
> The version from the current branch

REMOTE
> The version from the other branch

BASE
> The version from the merge base (common ancestor)

MERGED
> File to which the merged version should be written

The tool should exit with a code of zero to indicate that the user is happy with the merged version, saved to the filename in the MERGED environment variable. A nonzero exit code means that Git should ignore that file and not mark this conflict resolved. To define a new Git merge tool named "foo" with your own program named newtool:

```
[mergetool "foo"]
        cmd = newtool $LOCAL $REMOTE $MERGED $BASE
        trustExitCode = true
```

This shows the files being passed on the command line to new tool; if your program reads the environment variables itself, then of course that's not required. The trustExitCode setting means that Git will interpret the tool's exit code as previously described; if this setting is false, Git will prompt the user for what to do anyway.

Merge Strategies

Git has a number of approaches it can take to automatically merge files that have been changed by both sides of a merge; that is to say, exactly what it does in analyzing text to determine the boundaries of changed blocks, when blocks have been moved, when changes can be safely merged, and when they should be punted to the user. These approaches are called "merge strategies," and each may in turn have various options; Git can even be extended with new strategies by writing custom "merge drivers," without having to touch Git proper.

The built-in merge strategies are described in *git-merge(1)*. The many options are quite technical and involved, and Git's default choice of strategy is usually sufficient; we will not cover them in depth here. However, here are a few tips involving merge strategies that are generally useful:

`git merge -s ours`
> The ours strategy is simple: it discards all changes from the other branch. This leaves the content on your branch unchanged, and when you next merge from the other branch, Git will only consider changes made from this point forward. You might use this to retain the history of a branch, without incorporating its effects. (This strategy works with more than two branches as well.)

`git merge -s recursive -X ours`
> This is the ours option to the recursive strategy, not to be confused with the ours strategy. The recursive strategy is often the default, and so you might not have to use -s, but we'll be explicit here. This option directs Git to resolve conflicting changes in favor of the current branch. This is different from the ours strategy, in that nonconflicting changes can still be resolved in favor of either branch. You can use -X theirs as well, to resolve in favor of the other branch instead.

`ignore-space-change, ignore-all-space, ignore-space-at-eol`
> These options to the recursive strategy automatically resolve conflicts differing only in certain types of whitespace; see *git-merge(1)* for details.

`merge.verbosity`
> This configuration variable (or the GIT_MERGE_VERBOSITY environment variable, which takes precedence), holds a natural number indicating the level of information printed by the recursive strategy. Zero prints only a final error message

on conflict, 2 is the default, and 5 and above show debugging information.

The "octopus" strategy

The octopus strategy can merge any number of branches, but only if all changes can be resolved automatically. If not, the strategy will abort in the middle of the merge attempt, possibly leaving your index and working tree in a not terribly meaningful state. Unlike when merging two branches, `git merge --abort` doesn't work in this case (it says no merge is in progress); this may be a limitation that will be addressed in future versions of Git. You can use `git reset` to discard the index changes, adding `--hard` to reset the working tree as well, if you had no uncommitted changes to lose. "Octopus" is the default strategy when merging more than two branches, e.g., `git merge bert ernie oscar`.

Why the Octopus?

An octopus merge is generally used to tie together several topic branches with the master branch in preparation for a new release of a project, bringing in all their separate contributions. The individual branches should already have been reconciled with the master and have no conflicts amongst them, or else as mentioned, the octopus merge will not work. The octopus merge does not have any inherent advantage over simply merging all the topic branches into the master pairwise and reconciling the conflicts there; it accomplishes the same goal and incorporates the same history. However, with a large number of branches, it can make for a cleaner and more easily understood commit graph, and so some people prefer it. See Figure 7-1.

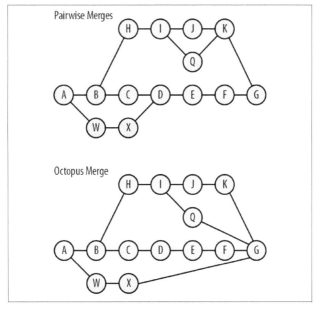

Figure 7-1. Pairwise and octopus merges

Reusing Previous Merge Decisions

Git can remember merge conflict resolutions you made in the past, and reuse them automatically if you run into similar conflicts later. This feature goes by the name `git rerere`, for "reuse recorded resolution." This is useful if you're working on a particularly difficult merge. You may abort a merge and retry it in various ways, but having resolved some conflicts in the meantime, this feature can remember and reapply those decisions. It can also be helpful if you're rewriting repository history, or in maintaining branches on which you end up resolving the same conflicts repeatedly until the branch's content can finally be merged appropriately.

Setting `rerere.enabled` in a repository turns on the feature, which is then automatically used by both `git merge` and `git rebase`. Since this is an advanced feature, we just note its existence here and refer the reader to *git-rerere(1)* for details.

## CHAPTER 8

Naming Commits

Git has a variety of ways to refer to (or name, or "spell") Git objects, usually commits, either individually or as a set, by following the commit graph or matching some criteria. You can find further detail on the conventions described next in *gitrevisions(7)*.

The command `git rev-parse` is useful for checking your understanding: it will take a name in the various syntaxes presented here and translate it to an object ID, so you can make sure it refers to the object you expected. For names that represent sets of commits, `git rev-list` will show the resulting set.

Naming Individual Commits

Commit ID

The full SHA-1 object ID
> For example, `2ee20b94203f22cc432d02cd5adb5ba610e6088f`.

An abbreviated object ID
> A prefix of an object's full ID unique to your repository. So `2ee20b94` could name the same object as before, if no other object in your database has an ID beginning with those digits (if there were a conflict, you could just use a few more digits).

`git describe`

> The output of the `git describe` command, which names commits relative to a tag; for example, `v1.7.12-146-g16d26b16` refers to commit 16d26b16, which is 146 commits away from the tag `v1.7.12`. As output, this might be used as part of a build identifier, where it suggests to the reader the proximity of the build to a tag with a presumably helpful name. As input to Git however, only the trailing hex digits after `-g` are meaningful, and are used as an abbreviated commit ID.

Ref Name

A simple ref points directly to an object ID. Git follows a symbolic ref such as "master" until it finds a simple ref; for example, HEAD points to *master* if you are that branch, and *master* points to the commit at the branch tip. If the object is a tag rather than a commit, then Git follows the tag (possibly through intermediate tags) until it reaches a commit.

There are several rules for expanding ref names, allowing you to use short names in most situations rather than fully qualified names such as `refs/heads/master`. To find a ref named `foo`, Git looks for the following in order:

1. `foo`: Normally, these are refs used by Git internally, such as HEAD, `MERGE_HEAD`, `FETCH_HEAD`, and so on, and are represented as files directly under *.git*

2. `refs/foo`

3. `refs/tags/foo`: The namespace for tags

4. `refs/heads/foo`: The namespace for local branches

5. `refs/remotes/foo`: The namespace for remotes, though this would not ordinarily itself be a ref, but rather a directory containing the remote's refs

6. `refs/remotes/foo/HEAD`: The default branch of the remote "foo"

Briefly, this means that `git checkout foo` will check out a tag named *foo* if there is one, otherwise, a branch; if there is neither, but there is a remote named *foo*, then it will check out the default branch of that remote.

Names Relative to a Given Commit

In the following, *rev* refers to any "revision": an object referred to using any of the syntaxes discussed in this chapter. These rules can apply multiple times; e.g., a tag name `tigger` is a rev, thus `tigger^` is also a rev, as is `tigger^^` (using the first rule that follows):

rev^n

> For example, `master^2`; this refers to the nth parent of a commit, numbered starting at 1. Recall from "The Object Store" on page 6 that a commit contains a list of zero or more parent commits, referred to by their object IDs; commits with more than one parent are produced by merging. Special cases:
>
> - `rev^` = `rev^1`
>
> - `rev^0` = `rev` if `rev` is a commit. If `rev` is a tag, then `rev^0` is the commit to which the tag refers, possibly through a chain of other tags (see `rev^{commit}` next).

In a linear history, `rev^` is the previous commit to `rev`, and `rev^^` the commit two steps back. Remember though that in the presence of merges, there may not be a single "previous commit," and these expressions may not do what you expect; for example, note carefully that, in Figure 8-1, `rev^^` ≠ `rev^2`.

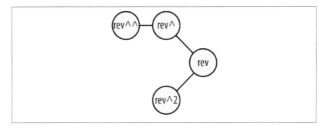

Figure 8-1. rev^^ vs rev^2

`rev~n`

> For example, `HEAD~3`; this is the nth ancestor of `rev`, always
> following the first parent commit. Special cases:
>
> - `rev~` = `rev~1`
>
> - `rev~0` = `rev`
>
> Again, be careful: `HEAD~2` = `HEAD^1^1` = `HEAD^^`, but these are
> *not* the same as `HEAD^2`.

Names Relative to the Reflog

Local branch names usually have a reflog: a log of commits that
used to be the head of this branch, along with the actions that
changed it each time: `commit`, `cherry-pick`, `reset`, and so on. You
view the composite log with `git log -g`, which follows your trail
from one branch log to another via checkouts. The syntax
`refname@{selector}` allows you to name a single commit according to various criteria evaluated against your reflog:

`refname@{time/date}`

> The commit named by this ref at the given point in time.
> The time can be specified in a very flexible format that does
> not appear to be documented in the man pages, but that
> includes such expressions as:
>
> - `now`
>
> - `yesterday`

- last week

- 6 months ago

- two Saturdays past

- `Sat Sep 8 02:09:07 2012 -0400` (or meaningful subsets of this)

- `1966-12-06 04:33:00`

Times after the latest commit return the latest commit, and similarly times previous to the earliest commit return the earliest commit. You can use dots instead of spaces to avoid having to quote or escape spaces to the shell, to ease typing: `topic@{last.week}` instead of `topic@{"last week"}` or `topic@{last\ week}`.

refname`@{`*n*`}`

For nonnegative *n*, this is the *n*th prior value of `refname` (zero refers to the current value and is a synonym for `refname`). Note that this need *not* be the same as *refname~n*, the *n*th prior commit on the branch! For example, if `git pull` performs a fast-forward update of a branch, there will be one entry in the reflog, but possibly several intervening commits. This is because Git added those commits in a single action; your branch moved from the previous commit to the last of the new ones in one step, and your branch was never "at" any of the intermediate ones (you never had them checked out).

You can omit `refname` to refer to the current branch (e.g., `@{5}`).

`@{`*-n*`}`

With a negative number, this is the current tip of the *n*th branch checked out before the current one. For example, if you're on *master* and switch to *foo* with `git checkout foo`, then `git checkout @{-1}` will take you back to *master*. Note the very different meanings of `@{5}` and `@{-5}`: the first is the fifth prior position of the current branch, while the latter is the fifth prior branch you checked out (and neither of them is HEAD~5 or HEAD^5). Also note the word "current" in this description: if the eighth prior branch you checked out was *master*, it probably had a different tip commit then, as reflected in the corresponding reflog entry—but this notation refers to the *current* tip of that branch. (You can't prefix this form with a ref name, as it is not relative.)

The critical thing to keep in mind about this syntax is that it is relative to *your* reflog, which is part of your repository and reflects your local work history; commits named this way are not globally meaningful or unique. Your reflog is a history of a particular branch *name* in your repository and the commits to which it has referred over time as a result of your checkouts, pulls, resets, amends, etc.; this is distinct from the history of the *branch* itself (a portion of the commit graph). The name master@{yester day}, for example, may refer to a different commit in your repository than in someone else's, even if you are working on the same project; it depends on what you were doing yesterday.

The Upstream Branch

The notation foo@{upstream} (or just foo@{u}) names the branch upstream of the branch *foo*, as defined by the repository configuration. This is usually arranged automatically when checking out a local branch corresponding to a remote one, but may be set explicitly with commands such as git checkout --track, git branch --set-upstream-to, and git push -u. It just gives the object ID of the upstream branch head, though; options to git rev-parse are useful to find out the upstream branch name:

```
$ git rev-parse HEAD@{upstream}
b801f8bf1a76ea5c6c6ac7addee2bc7161a79c93

$ git rev-parse --abbrev-ref HEAD@{upstream}
origin/master

$ git rev-parse --symbolic-full-name HEAD@{upstream}
refs/remotes/origin/master
```

The first is more convenient but may have difficulties if the branch name is ambiguous; Git will warn in that case. (See also the `strict` and `loose` arguments to `--abbrev-parse`.)

Matching a Commit Message

rev`^{/`*regexp*`}`

For example, `HEAD^{/"fixed pr#1234"}`; this selects the youngest commit reachable from `rev` whose commit message matches the given regular expression. You can omit `rev` by writing simply `:/`*regexp*; this selects the youngest matching commit reachable from *any* ref (branch or tag). A leading `!` is reserved (presumably for some sort of negation, though it does not yet have that meaning), so you have to repeat it as an escape if need be: `:/!!bang` searches for the string "!bang".

Notes

- Watch out for assuming that the commit you get is the one you want, especially if you omit `rev`; multiple commits might match your regular expression, and "youngest commit" means the one closest to the edge of the commit graph, which may not be the one with the most recent committer or author date. `git show -s` is useful to check that you have the right commit; omit the `-s` if you want to see the commit diff as well as the description (author, committer, date, and so on).

- The match is on the entire commit message, not just the subject, so the matching text itself may not show up if you use `git log --oneline` together with a match expression.

- You can't specify case-insensitive matching; if you want that, use `git log -i --grep`, which also uses the broader PCRE regular expressions rather than the simpler "regcomp" style used by the `:/` syntax.

Following Chains

There are various kinds of pointers or indirection in Git: a tag points to another object (usually a commit); a commit points to the tree representing the content of that commit; a tree points to its subtrees; and so on. The syntax *rev*^*type* tells Git to recursively dereference the object named by `rev` until it reaches an object of the given type. For example:

- `release-4.1^{commit}` names the commit tagged by `release-4.1`, even if there are intermediate tags.

- `master~3^{tree}` names the tree associated with the third commit back from the tip of the *master* branch.

You don't often have to use these kinds of names, as Git is smart about doing this automatically when appropriate. If you give a tag to `git checkout`, it knows you mean to check out the tagged commit; similarly, if you want to list the filenames in a commit, `git ls-tree -r master~3` would be sufficient. However, sometimes you need to be more precise: `git show release-4.1` would show both the tag and the commit; you could use `release-4.1^{commit}` to show only the commit. Special cases:

- *rev*^0 is a synonym for *rev*^{commit}.

- *rev*^{} means to follow the chain to the first nontag object (of whatever type).

Addressing Pathnames

The notation *rev*:*path* names a file by pathname in a given commit (e.g., `olympus@{last.week}:pantheon/zeus`). Actually, it's more general than that: recall from "The Object Store" on page 6 that a pathname *foo/bar/baz* names an object in some tree, either a blob (the contents of a file *baz*) or another tree (the entries in a directory *baz*). So `rev` can be any tree-like object: a tree (obviously), a commit (which has an associated tree), or the index,

---

and the object selected by `path` may be a blob (file) or another tree (directory). Special cases:

`:path`

> Addresses an object in the index.

`:n:path`

> Addresses an object in the index, including its stage number (see "Details on Merging" on page 105); `:path` is actually short for `:0:path`.

WARNING

Outside of Git, a filename such as *foo/bar*, without a leading slash, is relative to the current directory. In the notation `master:foo/bar`, however, it is *absolute* in the sense that it starts at the top of the tree of the named commit (the tip commit of the branch *master*, in this case). So if you're in the directory *foo* and want to see the version of *bar* two commits back, you might think to type `git show HEAD~2:bar` —but you'll get an error, or see the *bar* in the top level of the repository, if there is one.

To use relative pathnames in this notation, be explicit by using `./` or `../`; here, you need `git show HEAD~2:./bar` instead.

Naming Sets of Commits

The foregoing notation names individual commits. Git also allows you to name sets of commits, using a combination of reachability in the commit graph (containment in a branch or tag), and the usual mathematical operations on sets: union, intersection, complement, and difference. Here, the letters A, B, C, and so on are names for commits using any of the syntaxes introduced earlier. These terms can be used in combination, as a space-separated list of terms, and the definitions read as actions: adding or removing certain commits. Remember that a commit is always considered reachable from itself.

A

>   Add all commits reachable from A.

^A

>   Remove all commits reachable from A.

A^@

>   Add all commits reachable from A, but exclude A itself. This acts like a macro that expands to the list of parents of A, which are then interpreted according to (1).

A^!

>   Add only the commit A. This acts like a macro that expands A, followed by the list of A's parents each prefixed with a caret, which are then interpreted according to (1) and (2).

Since cases (3) and (4) can be expressed as combinations of (1) and (2), we can consider just the latter. To get a definition by sets for any expression, say:

    A ^X ^Y B C ^Z …

Rearrange to gather the T and ^T terms together:

    A B C … ^X ^Y ^Z …

And rewrite as:

    (A ∪ B ∪ C ∪ …) ∩ (X ∪ Y ∪ Z ∪ …)′

where each letter is interpreted as in (1), and the "prime" symbol (′) indicates the complement of a set in usual mathematical notation. If either category of term is absent, that union is the empty set; thus, if there are no caret terms, the intersection is with the complement of the empty set, that is, all commits—and so does not affect the result. Also, a term ^A by itself is meaningful and accepted, if not terribly useful: according to our definitions, this is the intersection of the empty set with the set of commits not reachable from A—that is, the empty set.

Here are some useful abbreviations:

```
--not X Y Z … = ^X ^Y ^Z …
A..B = ^A B
```
This is all commits reachable from B but not from A. Note that this excludes A itself.

```
A...B = A B --not $(git merge-base A B)
```
This is all commits reachable from either A or B, but not from both. It is called the *symmetric difference*, which is the name for the corresponding set operation: $(A \cup B) - (A \cap B)$.

For the .. and ... operators, a missing commit name on either side defaults to HEAD.

Here are some examples using this simple commit graph. See Figure 8-2.

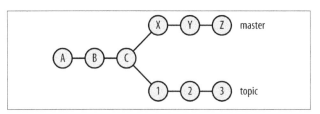

Figure 8-2. Simple commit graph

- **master** = {A, B, C, X, Y, Z}, the commits on the *master* branch

- **master..topic** = {1, 2, 3}, the commits on *topic* not yet merged into *master*

- **master...topic** = {1, 2, 3, X, Y, Z}, the commits by which the *topic* and *master* branches differ

A useful command for exploring this notation is git rev-list, which expands one of these expressions into the corresponding set of commits. It's especially helpful to combine it with git name-rev thus:

```
$ git rev-list rev | git name-rev --stdin --name-only
```

This will print out the commit set using names relative to local branches and tags.

WARNING

The use of this set notation depends on context. `git log` interprets its arguments just as shown in this section, indicating the set of commits on which it should report. `git checkout`, however, does not accept it, since it doesn't make sense to check out more than one commit at a time. And `git show` treats individual revs as naming just one commit (rather than all commits reachable from it), but accepts compound forms such as `A..B`.

Note too that `git diff` also uses the `..` and `...` syntaxes with pairs of commits—but with entirely different meanings! `git diff A..B` is just a synonym for `git diff A B`. Caveat Gittor.

## CHAPTER 9

Viewing History

The primary command for examining the commit history of your repository is git log. The documentation for this command, *git-log(1)*, is about 30 pages long, and we shall not repeat all that detail here. We will cover its main modes of operation, as well as a selection of the most common and useful options and techniques.

Command Format

The format of the command is:

```
$ git log [options] [commits] [[--] path ...]
```

The commits parameter specifies the commits Git should list for you, using the notation discussed in "Naming Sets of Commits" on page 123; for example:

git log

> The default for commits is HEAD, so this lists the commits reachable from the current HEAD commit. This is generally a branch, but may not be if you have checked out an arbitrary commit and are in "detached HEAD" mode (see "Branches" on page 19).

`git log topic`

> Lists the commits in the *topic* branch, even if you are on another branch.

`git log alvin simon`

> Lists all commits on either of the branches *alvin* or *simon*.

`git log alvin..simon`

> Lists all commits in *simon* that are not in *alvin*; this is often those commits on *simon* that have occurred since you last merged it with *alvin*.

Here, the names *topic*, *alvin*, and *simon* could also be tags, or expressions such as `master~3` or `780ae563`. You can also use patterns to indicate sets of refs instead of listing them all individually, with these options:

`--{branches,tags,remotes}[=pattern]`

> Behave as if all branches, tags, or remotes were given on the command line as the `commits` argument, optionally limiting the refs matched with a glob pattern. Match refs directly with `--glob=pattern`; a leading `refs/` is implied if not given. A trailing `/*` is implied if the pattern does not contain `*` or `?`.
>
> Synonyms: `--all = --glob='*'`

Thus, `git log --branches='foo*'` lists all branches whose names begin with "foo": `refs/heads/foobar`, `refs/heads/foodie`, etc.

The optional list of file pathnames or glob patterns further limits the commits listed, to those that touched matching paths by either adding, deleting, or modifying the named files. Use the `--` separator in case there's some ambiguity with the preceding options or commit names.

Output Formats

The default output format is fairly detailed, including the author timestamp and commit message:

```
$ git log
commit 86815742
Author: Richard E. Silverman <res@oreilly.com>
Date:   Tue Sep 18 14:36:00 2012 -0700

    reduce annoyance

    Fix this software so that it is slightly less
    annoying than it was before, though less annoyance
    would still be good.

commit 72e4d8e8
Merge: 5ac81f5f af771c39
Author: Witch King of Angmar <nazgul@barad-dur.org>
Date:   Tue Sep 18 14:35:54 2012 -0700

    Merge branch 'hobbits'

    Some scholars are of the opinion that "nazgûl" is
    exclusively plural, so that one does not speak of
    "a Nazgûl." Of course, it's best not to speak of
    them at all, regardless.
```

git log --oneline gives more compact output, including just
the ID and message subject for each commit:

```
$ git log --oneline
86815742 reduce annoyance
72e4d8e8 Merge branch 'hobbits'
...
```

Note that this is one reason to format your commit messages in
the conventional way, with a subject line: it makes this sort of
summary readable, as opposed to just showing the beginning of
a sentence trailing off to the right (see "Commit Messages" on
page 52).

The --oneline option is actually short for --format=oneline
--abbrev-commit, and the default is --format=medium. There are
a number of predefined formats; the following table shows the
full list, along with some commit elements they contain (they all
show the commit ID).

format	author	author date	committer	commit date	subject	message
oneline					✓	
short	✓				✓	
medium	✓	✓			✓	✓
full	✓		✓		✓	✓
fuller	✓	✓	✓	✓	✓	✓
email	✓	✓			✓	✓
raw	✓	✓	✓	✓	✓	✓

The email format produces output in traditional Unix "mbox" style, with one email message per commit (and here's yet another reason for the standard commit message format: commit subject lines become the email subject headers of each message). You can use it to prepare a set of email messages describing some commits, which can be easily read, manipulated, and sent with most Unix-based mail programs.

The raw format shows all the information in the commit in full detail and uninterpreted format, including the full 40-digit IDs of the parent commits and content tree object.

Defining Your Own Formats

You can also customize the display format, with git log --format ="format:*string*". You can give a format using a set of substitutions similar in usage to the printf function in the C standard library (and widely copied in other languages). The full set of substitutions is in the PRETTY FORMATS section of *git-log(1)*; here are some examples:

```
# committer, commit ID, relative timestamp, subject
$ git log --date=relative --format='%an, %h, %ar, "%s"
Richard E. Silverman, 86815742, 6 hours ago, "reduce …
Witch King of Angmar, 72e4d8e8, 7 hours ago, "Merge b…
...
```

This example uses color and underlining to distinguish the different fields on the line. The colors may not show here depending on the medium in which you're reading this text, but give it a try (it assumes your terminal is set up to handle color, of course):

```
# commit ID, subject, committer, date
$ git log --date=short --format=\
"%C(blue)%h %C(reset)%s %C(magenta)%aN %C(green ul)\
%ad%C(reset)"
86815742 reduce annoyance Richard E. Silverman 2012-1…
72e4d8e8 Merge branch 'hobbits' Witch King of Angmar …
...
```

Make sure to use %Creset at the end of such a format; otherwise, if the output is going directly to a terminal rather than through a pager, you'll leave the terminal stuck in whatever color or mode you last used. You can add a format you use frequently to your configuration in *~/.gitconfig* or elsewhere:

```
[pretty]
  colorful = "%C(blue)%h %C(reset)%s %C(magenta)%aN
  %C(green ul)%ad%C(reset)"
```

and then refer to it by name:

```
$ git log --format=colorful
```

Notes

- To use a double quote in a format string given in a Git configuration file, escape it with backslash.

- --pretty is a synonym for --format (from the term "pretty printing").

- A format given as format:*template* places a newline between each log item; there is no newline after the final item. Use tformat:*template* instead to get a final newline ("t" for "terminator").

- If the --format argument contains a percent sign (%), then Git assumes tformat:, as in the previous example.

- You can change the default format for `git log` by setting `format.pretty`; this affects `git show` as well.

Limiting Commits to Be Shown

There are many options for further limiting the commits to be shown beyond the *commits* expression given as an argument to `git log`; here is a selection of common ones:

`-n (-n n, --max-count=n)`
> Only show the first *n* commits.

`--skip=n`
> Skip *n* leading commits before starting output.

`--{before,after}=date`
> Show commits made before or after a specific date (synonyms: `--{until,since}`). Note that this refers to the commit timestamp; there is no analogous simple way to refer to the author timestamp.

`--{author,committer}=regexp`
> Show only commits whose author or committer header (`name <email>`) matches the given regular expression. Multiple instances of a given constraint are combined with logical "or," but (as usual) use of both types counts as logical "and"; thus, `git log --author=Richard --author=Booboo --committer=Felix` shows commits made by Felix, whose author is either Richard or Booboo.

`--grep=regexp`
> Show only commits whose log messages match the given regular expression. Multiple instances are combined with logical "or"; change this to "and" with `--all-match`. Use `--grep-reflog` to match reflog entries instead, when using `git log -g` to examine the reflog instead of the commit graph (`--grep` still matches the commit message, even though the commits examined are found via the reflog; it does not match the reflog comment instead).

`--{min,max}-parents=n`

> Show only commits with a matching number of parent commits. Synonyms:
>
> - `--merges` = `--min-parents=2`
>
> - `--no-merges` = `--max-parents=1`

`--first-parent`

> Follow only the first parent of a merge commit, rather than all of them. This can give a more useful history of a topic branch into which you periodically merge from a more central branch, keeping it up to date with the main development. This shows only the activity on the topic branch itself, rather than commits brought in from the main branch by merging.

`--diff-filter=[A|C|D|M|R|T]`

> Show commits containing files with any of the statuses given by the following one-letter codes. The "copied" and "renamed" statuses will only be effective if copy and rename detection are enabled as described:
>
> - `A`: Added
>
> - `C`: Copied
>
> - `D`: Deleted
>
> - `M`: Modified
>
> - `R`: Renamed
>
> - `T`: Type change (e.g., a file replaced by a symbolic link)

Regular Expressions

A number of options affect the interpretation of regular expressions:

`-i (--regexp-ignore-case)`

Ignore case differences (e.g., hello and HELLO will both match "Hello").

`-E (--extended-regexp)`

Use extended regular expressions; the default type is basic.

`-F (--fixed-strings)`

Consider the limiting patterns as literal strings to be matched; that is, don't interpret them as regular expressions at all.

`--perl-regexp`

Use Perl-style regular expressions. This will not be available if Git is not built with the `--with-libpcre` option, which is not on by default.

Reflog

`git log --walk-reflogs (-g)` shows a completely different log: the *reflog*. This is a log of actions you've taken in your repository, and it can be very helpful in recovering from mistakes; see "Double Oops!" on page 59.

Decoration

`git log --decorate={no,short,full}` shows refs pointing to the listed commits:

```
$ git log --decorate
commit feca033e (HEAD, master)
Author: Richard E. Silverman <res@oreilly.com>
Date:   Thu Dec 20 00:38:51 2012 -0500

    demo

commit 6faac5df (u/master, origin/master, origin/HEAD)
Author: Richard E. Silverman <res@oreilly.com>
Date:   Mon Dec 3 03:18:43 2012 -0500

    working on ch09
```

```
commit 110dac65
Author: Richard E. Silverman <res@oreilly.com>
Date:   Mon Dec 3 03:18:09 2012 -0500

    minor editing on earlier chapters
```

Note the inclusion in parentheses of various local and remote branch names. The default is short; full uses the full ref name (e.g., refs/heads/master instead of just master).

Date Style

git log --date= {local,relative,default,iso,rfc,short,raw}
> This option affects how dates are rendered in formatted log output, as long as the format has not explicitly given a date style. For example, using this format:

```
[pretty]
    compact = %h %ad, \"%s\"
```

```
$ git log -1 --format=compact --date=local
6faac5df Mon Dec 3 03:18:43 2012, "working on ch09"
```

```
$ git log -1 --format=compact --date=relative
6faac5df 2 weeks ago, "working on ch09"
```

```
$ git log -1 --format=compact --date=iso
6faac5df 2012-12-03 03:18:43 -0500, "working on ch09"
```

```
$ git log -1 --format=compact --date=rfc
6faac5df Mon, 3 Dec 2012 03:18:43 -0500, "working on …
```

```
$ git log -1 --format=compact --date=short
6faac5df 2012-12-03, "working on ch09"
```

```
$ git log -1 --format=compact --date=raw
6faac5df 1354522723 -0500, "working on ch09"
```

default
> Original time zone of author or committer

local
> Local time zone

relative
> How far in the past

iso
> ISO 8601 format

rfc
> RFC 2822 format (as found in email)

raw
> Internal Git format

Listing Changed Files

`git log --name-status` summarizes which files changed in a given commit (relative to its predecessor), and the nature of the changes:

```
$ git log --name-status
commit bc0ba0f7
Author: Richard E. Silverman <res@oreilly.com>
Date:   Wed Dec 19 23:31:49 2012 -0500

    fix directory; misc diffs with older ghc

M       keepmeta.hs

commit f6a96775
Author: Richard E. Silverman <res@oreilly.com>
Date:   Wed Dec 19 21:48:26 2012 -0500

    rename keepmeta

D       .gitfoo
A       Makefile
D       commit.hs
A       keepmeta.hs
```

The single-letter codes to the left of the filenames, indicating the change status of that file in the commit, are the same as listed for the `--diff-filter` option for added, deleted, modified, and so on.

`git log --name-only` lists only filenames without the status codes, and `--stat` gives an ASCII-art graph ("diffstat") representing the amount and kind of change in each file:

```
$ git log --stat
commit ddcd718b
Author: Richard E. Silverman <res@oreilly.com>
Date:   Sun Dec 9 23:47:50 2012 -0500

    add KDC default referral feature

    Two new realm configuration parameters:

    * default_referral_realm (string, none)
    * cross_realm_default_referral (boolean, false)

    If default_referral_realm is set, then the KDC
    will issue referrals to the specified realm for
    TGS requests otherwise qualifying for a referral
    but lacking a static realm mapping, as long as the
    presented TGT is not cross-realm (setting
    cross_realm_default_referral omits that check).

 src/config-files/kdc.conf.M | 12 +
 src/include/adm.h           |  4 +
 src/include/k5-int.h        |  2
 src/kdc/do_tgs_req.c        | 52 +----------
 src/kdc/extern.h            |  4 +
 src/kdc/main.c              | 12
 src/lib/kadm5/admin.h       |  5 -
 src/lib/kadm5/alt_prof.c    | 15 +
 8 files changed, 95 insertions(+), 11 deletions(-)
```

`git log --dirstat` summarizes the amount of change in subdirectories (it can take a number of parameters controlling how the summarization is done):

```
$ git log --dirstat
commit 4dd1530f (tag: mit-krb5-1.10.3, origin/MIT)
Author: Richard E. Silverman <res@oreilly.com>
Date:   Mon Jan 9 15:03:23 2012 -0500

    import MIT Kerberos 1.10.3
```

```
52.1% doc/
 6.0% src/lib/
12.4% src/windows/identity/doc/
 3.7% src/windows/identity/ui/
 8.8% src/windows/identity/
 3.5% src/windows/leash/htmlhelp/
 3.4% src/windows/leash/
 9.5% src/
```

Showing and Following Renames or Copies

Ordinary git log does not show file renaming, because it takes longer to do this and often you're not interested. To enable renaming detection, use --find-renames[=*n*] (-M[*n*]). The optional integer *n* is an index of similarity: consider a delete/add pair to be a rename if the before/after files are at least *n*% identical (the default is 100%):

```
$ git log --name-status
commit 4a933304 (HEAD, master)
Author: Richard E. Silverman <res@qoxp.net>
Date:   Thu Dec 20 01:08:14 2012 -0500

    Rename foo; wouldn't bar be better?

D       foo
A       bar

$ git log --name-status -M
commit 4a933304 (HEAD, master)
Author: Richard E. Silverman <res@qoxp.net>
Date:   Thu Dec 20 01:08:14 2012 -0500

    Rename foo; wouldn't bar be better?

R100    foo     bar
```

To have Git follow a file past a rename, use git log --follow; this only works when you give a single file to follow:

```
$ git log bar
commit 4a933304 (HEAD, master)
Author: Richard E. Silverman <res@oreilly.com>
Date:    Thu Dec 20 01:08:14 2012 -0500

    Rename foo; wouldn't bar be better?

$ git log --follow bar
commit 4a933304 (HEAD, master)
Author: Richard E. Silverman <res@oreilly.com>
Date:    Thu Dec 20 01:08:14 2012 -0500

    Rename foo; wouldn't bar be better?

commit 4e286d96
Author: Richard E. Silverman <res@oreilly.com>
Date:    Tue Dec 18 04:57:55 2012 -0500

    Add "foo" in its glorious fooness!
```

Detecting Copies

A "copied" file is a new path appearing in a commit with identical or similar contents to an existing one (one already in a prior commit). git log --find-copies[=n] (-C[n]) does the same for detecting copies as -M does for renames. -CC (or --find-copies-harder) will consider all files in a commit as potential sources of copying, while plain -C considers only files that changed in that commit.

Rewriting Names and Addresses: The "mailmap"

The same person's name or email address as embedded in commits may vary in a single repository history, depending on settings she had at various times as she was working. Git has a facility to normalize these for display and collation, called the *mailmap*. A mailmap file may be named *.mailmap* at the top of the working tree, or have any name given by the mailmap.file configuration option, and has lines in any of the following formats:

```
Correct Name <user@foo.com>
```
This collates by address and rewrites names: entries of this form with the same address identify commits marked with those addresses as being by the same person, with the specified name replacing the names given in those commits.

```
<desired@email.address> <random@other.address>
```
This collates by address and rewrites addresses: entries of this form with the same desired address, but differing "random other" addresses, identify commits by the varying addresses as being by the same person, with the specified address replacing those appearing in the commits (but leaving the names alone).

```
Correct Name <desired@email.com> <random@other.org>
```
This collates by address and rewrites both name and address: entries of this form, with the same desired address but differing names and other addresses, identify those commits as being by the same person, with the specified name and desired address replacing those appearing in the commits.

```
Correct Name <desired@email.com> Other Name <random@oth
er.org>
```
This collates by both name and address, and rewrites both as well: entries of this form with the same "correct name" and desired address identify commits marked with the given combinations of "other" name/address pairs as being by the same person, with the specified name and address replacing those appearing in the commits.

For example, this mailmap entry:

```
Richard E. Silverman <res@oreilly.com>
```

coalesces all commits marked with the address res@oreilly.com and presents my name consistently as "Richard E. Silverman," even if some say "Richard Silverman" or "Rich S." These entries:

```
Richard E. Silverman <res@qoxp.net> <res@oreilly.com>
Richard E. Silverman <res@qoxp.net> <slade@shore.net>
Richard E. Silverman <res@qoxp.net> <rs@wesleyan.edu>
```

identify commits marked with the three addresses appearing on the right, and rewrite both name and address to be "Richard E. Silverman" and `res@qoxp.net`.

The coalescing and rewriting features are used by the command `git shortlog`, which summarizes history using the commit subjects (or other format given by `--format`) and grouping by author. The rewriting feature alone is used by `git log` and `git blame` if the format specifies it. Particular escapes for committer and author info, given in the PRETTY FORMATS section of *git-log(1)*, take the mailmap (if any) into account; for example, this version of the "compact" format defined earlier:

```
[pretty]
        compact = %aN (%h) %aD, \"%s\"
```

(note the capital N and D) shows the author name and address as rewritten by the mailmap.

Shortening Names

Another use for the mailmap is shortening names for compact display. Full names can be truncated and difficult to read in a short format, such as the common `git log --oneline`. You can maintain a mailmap rewriting full names to your organization's computer account names, for example, which are typically shorter. You can then define log formats that use them as above; you could place these in the system-level Git configuration used by everyone (usually */etc/gitconfig*), or have a smaller group explicitly include a shared file via the `include.path` variable. This mailmap:

```
res <res@example.com>
res <rsilverman@example.com>
john <jpreston@example.com>
john <john@example.com>
```

together with the second "compact" log format above causes the author name and addresses for Richard Silverman and John Preston to appear as "res" and "john" instead, also taking into account two different email address formats.

Searching for Changes: The "pickaxe"

The Git "pickaxe," `git log -S` *string*, lists commits that changed the number of occurrences of `string` in at least one file. Note that this is slightly different from `string` appearing in the commit diff at all: if a commit removed one occurrence and added another one elsewhere, the pickaxe will not show it. Nonetheless, this is a useful method of looking for changes. For example, if you want to know when a particular feature was added, using this command with the name of a function or variable specific to the feature will turn it up, as the earliest commit that introduced that term. `git log -G` *pattern* does the same with a regular expression.

If you combine the pickaxe with a `git log` option that lists files, such as `--name-status`, Git shows only those files that triggered the listing (those in which the number of string or pattern occurrences changed). If you add `--pickaxe-all`, then Git shows *all* files touched by the listed commits. This allows you to see the entire changeset associated with any commit that matched the pattern you're interested in.

Showing Diffs

`git log -p` shows the "patch" or "diff" associated with each commit (illustrating the actual changes made to the files, only for text files, naturally), after the usual commit information as indicated by the log format in use. Normally, no diff is shown for merge commits, however you can use these options:

`-m`
> Shows each pairwise diff between the merge and its parents.

`-c`

> Shows the differences with all parents simultaneously in a merged format (a generalization of the traditional "unified diff"), rather than serially as with `-m`, and only for files that were modified in all branches.

`--cc`

> Implies `-c` and further simplifies the diff by showing only conflicts; change regions with only two variants of which the merge picked one unmodified are not shown.

Color

The option `--color[={always,auto,never}]` uses color to help distinguish difference regions; additions are in green and deletions in red. The default is never, `--color` means `--color=always`, and `--color=auto` means to use color when standard output is a terminal.

Word Diff

The option `--word-diff[={plain,color,none}]` shows word-level changes within lines, rather than entire changed lines. For example, this:

```
- I changed a word.
+ I altered a word.
```

becomes this:

```
I [-changed-]{+altered+} a word.
```

with `--word-diff=plain`. This is often more useful than line diffs if the content is English prose rather than software code. The color option uses color instead of the markers shown earlier to indicate the additions and deletions, again using green and red. It is possible to change the regular expression Git uses to determine word boundaries with `--word-diff-regex`; see *git-log(1)* for details.

Comparing Branches

Often we are interested in understanding the relationship between the content of two branches, particularly in how they have diverged. As discussed in "Naming Sets of Commits" on page 123, a basic tool for this is the symmetric difference A...B, which shows those commits in either branches *A* or *B* but not in both (i.e., those commits added to either branch since they last diverged). Sometimes this isn't enough, though. For example, git cherry-pick creates a new commit based on an existing one, by reapplying the changes introduced by the original commit at a different place in the history. It is useful in situations where incorporating changes by merging is inconvenient or impossible due to repository organization. If a commit has been cherry-picked from one branch to another, then it will be included in their symmetric difference anyway, since they are distinct commits that just happen to represent the same changeset. git log --cherry-pick takes this into account by omitting commits that have identical diffs. Consider the commit graph in Figure 9-1, in which commit *2* was produced with git cherry-pick D on the *other* branch, and so it and *D* have the same changeset.

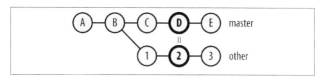

Figure 9-1. git log and cherry-picking

Assuming all the other commits have distinct changesets, we will see something like:

```
$ git log master...other
e5feb479 E
070e87e5 D
9b0e3dc5 C
6f70a016 3
0badfe94 2
15f47204 1
```

Whereas this omits the patch-equivalent commits, showing just content differences:

```
$ git log --cherry-pick master...other
e5feb479 E
9b0e3dc5 C
6f70a016 3
15f47204 1
```

The variation --cherry-mark will mark duplicate commits with an equal sign, instead of omitting them:

```
$ git log --cherry-mark master...other
+ e5feb479 E
= 070e87e5 D
+ 9b0e3dc5 C
+ 6f70a016 3
= 0badfe94 2
+ 15f47204 1
```

Displaying Sides

git log master..other (with just two dots) shows one side of this situation: those commits on *other* that are not on *master*. If you want cherry-pick detection, you have to consider both sides as before, but then you are no longer viewing just one side. You can recover this by adding --{left,right}-only:

```
$ git log master..other
6f70a016 3
0badfe94 2
15f47204 1

$ git log --cherry-pick --right-only master...other
6f70a016 3
15f47204 1
```

This shows commits on *other* that are not contained in *master* or patch-equivalent to another commit in their difference, in this case, omitting commit *2* since it is equivalent to *D*. And similar to --cherry-mark, the related option --left-right displays the side of a commit with the symbols < and >:

```
$ git log --cherry-mark --left-right master...other
< e5feb479 E
< 070e87e5 D
= 9b0e3dc5 C
> 6f70a016 3
= 0badfe94 2
> 15f47204 1
```

The simple option `--cherry` is a synonym for `--right-only`
`--cherry-mark --no-merges`, so that this:

```
$ git log --cherry HEAD@{upstream}...
```

shows the commits on your side of the current branch (ignoring
possible merges with other branches), marking those that duplicate changes made by distinct commits on the other side (prob-
able `cherry-picks`, either literally or by another means such as
applying patches via email with `git format-patch` and `git am`).

Showing Notes

`git log --notes[=ref]` includes any notes on a commit after its
message; see "git notes" on page 182 for how this command and Git
notes work in general.

Commit Ordering

Normally, `git log` displays commits in reverse chronological order according to the committer (not author) timestamps. You can
alter this in three ways:

- `--date-order` shows all children before their parents;

- `--topo-order` (for "topological") implies `--date-order`,
  and also groups commits from the same b ranch together;
  and

- `--reverse` reverses the output list.

History Simplification

Git has a number of options for pruning sections of history according to various notions of equivalence between parent and child commits, documented in the "History Simplification" section of *git-log(1)*. Since these are fairly specialized and abstruse, useful mostly with very large and complex histories, and well documented in the man page, we do not cover them here.

Related Commands

git cherry

```
git cherry [-v] [upstream [head [limit]]]
```

This command is similar to `git log --cherry`, but more specialized. It shows commits on a branch that are not in the upstream, marking those whose changes are duplicated by distinct upstream commits with a minus sign (while other commits have a plus sign). Using the same example as before, if we're on the *other* branch for which *master* is upstream:

```
$ git cherry -v --abbrev
+ 6f70a016 3
```

```
- 0badfe94 2
+ 15f47204 1
```

This shows that we have three new commits on our side, but the changes from commit 2 are already applied upstream (the -v option includes the commit message subject line). As shown, you can give specific current (*head*) and upstream branches for comparison, and also a limit commit so that only commits in `lim it..head` are eligible to be shown. The limit would be an earlier commit on the *head* branch, past which you are not interested in looking. The default is equivalent to `git cherry HEAD@{up stream} HEAD` (no limit).

git shortlog

As mentioned earlier, `git shortlog` summarizes commit history, grouping commits by author with the number of commits and their subjects, and applying a mailmap if available to rewrite author names or email addresses:

```
$ git shortlog
Ammon Riley (1):
      Make git-svn branch patterns match complete URL

Amos King (2):
      Do not name "repo" struct "remote" in push_http…
      http-push.c: use a faux remote to pass to http_…

Amos Waterland (6):
      tutorial note about git branch
      Explain what went wrong on update-cache of new …
      Do not create bogus branch from flag to git bra…
      git rebase loses author name/email if given bad…
      AIX compile fix for repo-config.c
      wcwidth redeclaration
   ...
```

This can be useful in preparing the release notes for a new version of a project, automatically collating the new features in this release. You could limit it to just the features since the last version by referring to the tags for the previous and current release (e.g., `git shortlog v1.0..v1.1`).

## CHAPTER 10

Editing History

In this chapter, we cover various techniques for editing repository history. Earlier chapters covered simple cases of this, focused on correcting individual commits; here, we're concerned with larger changes: moving branches, merging or splitting repositories, systematically altering an entire history, and so on.

The caution given earlier bears repeating here: you should not generally use any of these techniques on history that has already been published to other people! It will break their ability to use the push/pull mechanism, which may be very difficult and awkward to recover from. Only use these on private repositories, or if you can coordinate the change with everyone involved. It's easiest if all users of a shared repository commit and push all their outstanding changes, then simply reclone it after you make your edits. Or, they can use `git rebase` instead as we are about to describe, if they're a bit more adventurous.

Rebasing

We have already covered special cases of rebasing, especially for editing a sequence of commits at a branch tip; here, we consider the general case. The general purpose of `git rebase` is to move a branch from one location to another. Since commits are immutable, they can't actually be moved (their parent commits would change), so this entails making new commits with the same changesets and metadata: author, committer, timestamps, and so on. The steps Git follows during a rebase are as follows:

1. Identify the commits to be moved (more accurately, replicated).

2. Compute the corresponding changesets (patches).

3. Move HEAD to the new branch location (base).

4. Apply the changesets in order, making new commits preserving author information.

5. Finally, update the branch ref to point to the new tip commit.

The process of making new commits with the same changesets as existing ones is called "replaying" those commits. Step 4 can be modified with an "interactive rebase" (`git rebase --interactive (-i)`), allowing you to edit the commits in various ways as you move them; see the earlier discussion of this feature ("Editing a Series of Commits" on page 64).

The most general form of the command is:

```
$ git rebase [--onto newbase] [upstream] [branch]
```

which means to replay the commit set `upstream..branch` starting at `newbase`. The defaults are:

upstream: `HEAD@{upstream}`
    The upstream of the current branch, if any

branch:
    HEAD

newbase:
    The `upstream` argument, whatever its default or user-supplied value is

For example, given the commit graph in Figure 10-1, the command `git rebase --onto C master topic` would move the *topic* branch as shown in Figure 10-2.

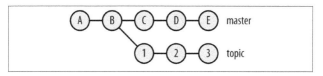

Figure 10-1. Before rebasing

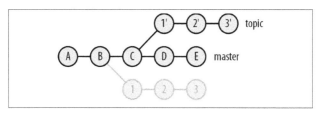

Figure 10-2. After rebasing

1′, 2′, and 3′ are new commits replicating the changesets of commits 1, 2, and 3. Calling B the "base" of the original (unmerged portion of) the *topic* branch, this changes the base from B to C, thus "rebasing" the branch.

The behavior of the default arguments to `git rebase` reveals the simplest use of rebasing: keeping a sequence of local commits at the tip of a branch as the upstream progresses, rather than performing a merge. After doing a `git fetch`, you see that your local *master* branch has diverged from its upstream counterpart (see Figure 10-3).

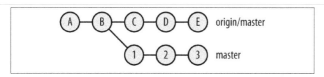

Figure 10-3. Before rebasing

Following the preceding defaults, the simple command:

```
$ git rebase
```

actually means:

```
$ git rebase --onto origin/master origin/master master
```

which in turn means to replay the commit set `origin/master..master` at `origin/master`, resulting in the change shown in Figure 10-4.

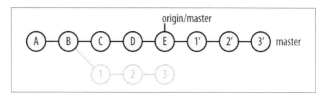

Figure 10-4. After rebasing

Your local commits 1, 2, and 3 have been shifted forward to remain based off the tip of the upstream *master*. This is such a common use of rebasing for certain workflows that there is a `--rebase` option to `git pull` that runs `git rebase` in between its fetch and merge steps (see "Pull with Rebase" on page 89). In this case, the final step merging *origin/master* into *master* will do nothing, since if the rebase is successful, the upstream branch *origin/master* is now already contained in the local *master*.

Undoing a Rebase

The final step of a successful rebase is to repoint the ref of the branch being moved, from the old tip commit to the new one. The original commits are not immediately expunged in any way, but merely abandoned: they are no longer reachable in the commit graph from any branch, and will be garbage collected by Git if they remain that way for some time. To undo the rebase operation, then, all you need to do is move the branch ref back to its original spot, which you can discover using the reflog. After the `git rebase`, for example, your reflog would look something like this:

```
$ git log -g
b61101ac HEAD@{0}: rebase finished: returning to
refs/heads/master
b61101ac HEAD@{1}: rebase: 3
6f554c9a HEAD@{2}: rebase: 2
cb7496ab HEAD@{3}: rebase: 1
baa5d906 HEAD@{4}: checkout: moving from master to
baa5d906...
e3a1d5b0 HEAD@{5}: commit: 3
```

The checkout step is the beginning of the rebase as Git moves
HEAD to the new base, the tip of the upstream *origin/master*
(here at commit baa5d906). The rebase steps replay commits 1,
2, and 3 at the new location, and in the final step, the local *master* branch (full ref name refs/heads/master) is reset to the new
tip commit. In the earliest reflog entry, you can see when you
made your original version of commit 3, with commit ID
e3a1d5b0. To return to that state, all you need to do is:

```
$ git reset --hard e3a1d5b0
```

The original tip commit might not be at the same spot as shown
here, since that depends on the exact sequence of commands you
used, but it will show up somewhere earlier in the reflog.

Importing from One Repository to Another

Suppose you would like to combine two repositories—say, to
import the entire content of repository *B* as a subdirectory *b* of
repository *A*. You could just copy the working tree of *B* into *A*
and then add and commit it, of course, but you want to retain the
history of repository *B* as well as the content. Though that's easy
to say, it's not immediately clear what this means. The Git history
of each repository consists of an entire graph of individual content snapshots, branching and merging in possibly complex ways
over time, and there are different ways in which you might want
to combine the two. In this section, we discuss a few of them.

Importing Disconnected History

The simplest way to combine two repositories is simply to import the whole commit graph of one into the other, without connecting them in any way. Ordinarily, a repository has a single "root commit," that is, a commit with no parents—the first commit created after the repository was initialized, of which all other commits are descendants. However, there is nothing preventing you from having multiple root commits in a single repository, in which case the commit graph consists of multiple disconnected regions; in Figure 10-5, commits A and 1 are both root commits.

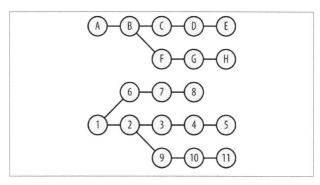

Figure 10-5. Multiple root commits

Here's how to import repository *B* into repository *A* in this fashion:

```
$ cd A
$ git remote add B URL
$ git fetch B
warning: no common commits
...
 [new branch]      master     -> B/master
 [new branch]      zorro      -> B/zorro
$ git for-each-ref --shell \
   --format='git branch --no-track %(refname:short)
   %(refname:short)' \
   'refs/remotes/B/*' | sed -e 's:/:-:' | sh -x
```

```
$ git branch
  B-master
  B-zorro
  master
$ git remote rm B
```

This recipe uses `git for-each-ref`, a versatile tool for generating scripts on the fly that apply to a given set of refs (in this case, branches). For each named ref, here selected by the pattern `refs/remotes/B/*` (all tracking branches for the remote B), it generates a separate `git branch` command substituting the names marked with `%(…)` to reflect that ref. This series of commands then goes through the Unix command *sed* rewriting `B/foo` to `B-foo`, and finally, the commands are run by feeding them into the Bourne shell (*sh*). (See *git-for-each-ref(1)* for more detail on this handy command for Git automation.)

The case of pulling in a completely disconnected commit graph is sufficiently unusual that Git warns you about it, saying that the repository you're fetching has "no common commits" with this one.

After the `fetch` command, Git has copied the entire commit graph of *B* into the object database of *A*, but the only references in *A* to the new branches are remote-tracking ones: `B/master` and `B/zorro`. To finish incorporating *B* into *A*, we need to make local branches for these. The `git for-each-ref` incantation prepares and runs a set of Git commands that create a local branch named *B-x* for each remote branch *B/x*, by running `git branch --no-track B-x B/x`. The `--no-track` option avoids creating unnecessary tracking relationships that would just be removed later. We prefix the new branch names with *B-*, since there may be clashes (as here, where there is a *master* branch in each repository). Finally, when done, we remove the remote *B*, since we do not intend to continue tracking the other repository; the remote was just a mechanism to perform the import.

This demonstrates a general way of doing it; you can of course just run the appropriate `git branch` commands yourself to name the new branches as you wish, if there are few of them, or rename them afterward with `git branch -m *old new*`.

Although this is the easiest method of combining two histories, it is also not usually what you want to do, because you can't use the Git merge mechanism on branches that were originally part of distinct histories. This is because `git merge` looks for a "merge base": a common ancestor commit of the branches being merged —and in this case, there is no such commit. You might use this technique if you have rearranged the history of a repository, but want to keep the original history around for reference, and it's more convenient to have it both in one repository than split over two.

Importing Linear History

To import history so that it is connected to the commit graph of the receiving repository, you can't just use the existing commits of the donor repository as before, since you need new parent commit pointers to connect the two histories and you can't actually change commits. Instead, you must make new commits introducing the same content (as with `git rebase`). If the history you want to import is linear—either the entire repository, or the branch you're interested in—then you can use `git format-patch` and `git am` to do this easily (these commands are described more fully in "Patches with Commit Information" on page 170). Here's a formula for adding the complete history of branch *foo* in repository *B* to the current branch in repository *A*:

```
$ cd A
$ git --git-dir /path/to/B/.git format-patch --root ↵
--stdout foo | git am
```

This formats the commits on branch *foo* in repository *B* as a series of patches with accompanying metadata (author, committer, timestamps, and so on), and feeds that into `git am`, which applies the patches as new commits in repository *A*. Note that you can't refer to *B* here directly as a remote repository with a URL; you need a local copy to use, for which you can just clone *B* and check out the branch you want to import.

Because you are now applying patches rather than importing commits whole, you might encounter conflicts if the source and destination repositories have overlapping content (the same filenames). To avoid this, you can tell git am to prepend a directory to all filenames with --directory, thus depositing the files in the imported history inside a new directory. Combined with the -p*n* option, which first removes *n* leading directories from those filenames, and with limiting the source files via an argument to git format-patch, you can import a particular directory or other subset of files into a new directory without conflicts. Extending the preceding example:

```
$ cd A
$ git --git-dir /path/to/B/.git format-patch --root ↵
--stdout foo -- src | git am -p2 --directory dst
```

This imports the history on the branch *foo* in repository *B*, limited to files in the directory *src*, and places those files in directory *dst* instead in repository *A*.

Without --root, just giving a rev foo means foo..HEAD: the recent commits on the current branch that are not in the history of *foo*. You can also give a range expression of your own to specify the commits to include (e.g., 9ec0eafb..master).

WARNING

If the source branch history is not linear (contains merge commits), git format-patch won't complain; it will just produce patches for all the nonmerge commits. This is likely to cause conflicts; see the next section.

Importing Nonlinear History

Because the git format-patch/git am technique works only on a linear source history, here is a recipe for importing a branch with a nonlinear history, using git rebase instead. You can use the present procedure on linear history as well, if you find the previous one too slow or unwieldy (as it might be; it's simpler, but it's not what those commands are really intended to do).

The following example adds the history of the branch *isis* in a remote repository to the tip of the current branch in this one (here, the *master* branch):

```
# Add the source repository as a temporary remote
# named "temp".
$ git remote add temp URL
# Fetch the branch "isis" from the remote.
$ git fetch temp isis
...
* branch              isis       -> FETCH_HEAD
# Make a local branch named "import" for the remote
# branch we want to bring in.
$ git branch import FETCH_HEAD
# Replay the "import" branch commits on the current
# branch, preserving merges.
$ git rebase --preserve-merges --root --onto HEAD import
...
Successfully rebased and updated refs/heads/import.
# Finally, fast-forward the local branch (master) to
# its new tip (where "import" is now), and remove the
# temporary branch and remote.
$ git checkout master
Switched to branch 'master'
$ git merge import
Updating dffbfac7..6193cf87
Fast-forward
...
$ git branch -d import
Deleted branch import (was 6193cf87).
$ git remote rm temp
```

This technique copies the source branch into the current repository under a temporary name, uses git rebase to graft it onto the tip of the current branch, then moves the local branch up to its new tip and deletes the temporary import branch.

Unfortunately, git rebase lacks the capabilities provided by the various arguments and options to git format-patch and git am shown earlier, which let you relocate files as you import to avoid pathname conflicts. To get the same result, you'll need to clone the source repository and rearrange it first before importing from it. The section "The Big Hammer: git filter-branch" on page 162 shows how to do this.

Commit Surgery: git replace

Sometimes, you really just need to replace a single commit—but it's buried in the middle of a complex history with multiple branches that would be difficult to rewrite using git rebase -i. For example, suppose you accidentally used the wrong committer name at one point, perhaps because you had GIT_COMMIT TER_NAME set and forgot to change it for this repository with git config user.name:

```
$ git log --format='%h %an'
...
0922daf4 Richard E. Silverman
6426690c Richard E. Silverman
03f482d6 Bozo the Clown
27e9535f Richard E. Silverman
78d481d3 Richard E. Silverman
...
```

Git has a command, git replace, which allows you to perform "commit surgery" by replacing any commit with a different one, without disturbing the commits around it. Now, your first instinct at this point should be to say, "That's impossible"; we've explained before that because commits point to their parents, it's impossible to alter a commit that has children without recursively altering all commits after that point in the history as well. That's still true, and git replace is actually a trick, as we'll see.

To fix commit 03f482d6, we first check it out and amend it with the correct author name, creating the new commit we want to use as a replacement:

```
$ git checkout 03f482d6
Note: checking out '03f482d6'.

You are in 'detached HEAD' state...
```

```
$ git commit --amend --reset-author -C HEAD
[detached HEAD 42627abe] add big red nose
...
```

Now we have a new commit, 42627abe, which has the same content and parents as the faulty commit (and now, the correct author name). It is sitting off to the side on the commit graph shown in Figure 10-6.

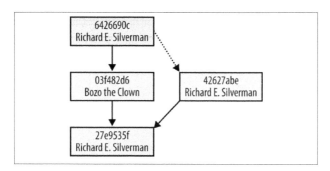

Figure 10-6. Replacing a commit

And now we just need to get commit 6426690c to "believe" that it has 42627abe as a parent instead of 03f482d6. The magic command is:

```
$ git replace 03f482d6 42627abe
```

And now, after returning to the original location (say, *master*), we see this:

```
$ git log --format='%h %an'
...
0922daf4 Richard E. Silverman
6426690c Richard E. Silverman
03f482d6 Richard E. Silverman
27e9535f Richard E. Silverman
78d481d3 Richard E. Silverman
...
```

This is, quite simply, a lie. This log claims that commit 03f482d6 now has a different author but the same commit ID, which is effectively impossible. What has happened is that `git replace` manages a list of object replacements, recorded in the namespace `refs/replace`; the name of a ref there is the ID of an object to replace, and its referent is the ID of the replacement:

```
$ git show-ref | grep refs/replace
42627abe6d4b1e19cb55… refs/replace/03f482d654930f7aa1…
```

While Git operates, whenever it retrieves the contents of an object in the object database it checks the replacement list first, and silently substitutes the contents of the replacement object, if any. Thus, in the preceding example, Git still displays the original commit ID, but shows the corrected author (which is in the content of the replacement commit).

Keeping It Real

The replacement list is an artifact of your repository; it alters your view of the commit graph, but not the graph itself. If you were to clone this repository or push to another one, the replacement would not be visible there. To make it "real," we have to actually rewrite all the subsequent commits, which you can do thus:

```
$ git filter-branch -- --all
```

but see the next section on `git filter-branch` for more on that command.

The usual workflow with this feature, then, is as follows:

1. Use `git replace` to make the commit graph appear as you want it.

2. Use `git filter-branch` to reify the change.

3. Push the changes elsewhere, if necessary.

You probably don't want to push while you have replacements in force, since you don't really know what you're pushing!

The Big Hammer: git filter-branch

`git filter-branch` is the most general tool for altering the history of a repository. It walks the portion of the commit graph you specify (by default, the current branch), applying various filters you supply and rewriting commits as necessary. You can use it to make wholesale programmatic alterations to the entire history. Since this is an advanced command, we will just sketch its operation and refer the reader to *git-filter-branch(1)* for more detail.

You can apply the following filters, whose string arguments are passed to the shell. When they run, the environment contains the following variables reflecting the commit being rewritten:

- GIT_COMMIT (commit ID)
- GIT_AUTHOR_NAME

- GIT_AUTHOR_EMAIL

- GIT_AUTHOR_DATE

- GIT_COMMITTER_NAME

- GIT_COMMITTER_EMAIL

- GIT_COMMITTER_DATE

The filters are:

`--env-filter`
> Modifies the environment in which the commit will happen (e.g., you can change the author name by setting and exporting GIT_AUTHOR_NAME).

`--tree-filter`
> Modifies commit contents by altering the working tree. Git treats the resulting tree as if you had run `git add -Af`, reflecting all new and deleted files while ignoring the usual "ignore" rules in *.gitignore* and so on.

`--index-filter`
> Modifies commit contents by altering the index. If you can effect the changes you want solely by manipulating the index, then this is much faster than `--tree-filter` since it does not have to check out the working tree. We give an example of this in "Expunging Files" on page 165.

`--parent-filter`
> Modifies the commit's parent list, transforming the list from stdin to stdout. The list is in the format specified by *git-commit-tree(1)*.

`--msg-filter`
> Modifies the commit message, transforming the message from stdin to stdout.

`--commit-filter`
> Git runs this instead of the normal `git commit-tree` to actually perform the commit.

`--tag-name-filter`
> Transforms the names of tags pointing to rewritten objects from stdin to stdout.

The value of this option is not a shell command, but rather a directory name:

`--subdirectory-filter`
> Consider only history relevant to the given directory, and rewrite pathnames to make it the new project root. This creates a new history containing only files in that directory, with it as the new top of the repository.

As a hedge against mistakes, `git filter-branch` stores the original branch refs in the namespace `refs/original` (which you can change with `--original`). It will refuse to overwrite existing original refs without `--force`.

The arguments to `git filter-branch` are interpreted as by `git rev-list`, selecting the commits to be visited; to use arguments beginning with hyphens, separate them from the filter-branch options with `--` as usual. For example, the default argument is HEAD, but you can rewrite all branches with one command: `git filter-branch -- --all`.

It does not make sense to specify commits to rewrite by commit ID:

```
$ git filter-branch 27e9535f
Which ref do you want to rewrite?
```

because when done, `git filter-branch` needs to update an existing ref to point to the rewritten branch. Ordinarily, you will give a branch name. If you limit the commit range using the negation of a ref, such as `master..topic` (equivalent to `^master topic`), then only the refs mentioned in the positive sense will be updated; here, Git will visit the commits on *topic* that are not on *master*, but update only the *topic* branch when done.

Examples

Expunging Files

Suppose you discover that you have accidentally littered your history with some cruft, such as *.orig and *.rej files from patching, or *~ backup files from Emacs. You can expunge all such files from your entire project history with this command:

```
$ git filter-branch --index-filter ↵
'git rm -q --cached --ignore-unmatch *.orig *.rej ↵
*~' -- --all
```

You might then add these patterns to your ignore rules, to prevent this from happening again.

Shifting to a Subdirectory

This recipe (using *bash* syntax) shifts the root of the current project into a subdirectory named *sub*:

```
$ git filter-branch ↵
--index-filter ↵
'git ls-files -s | perl -pe "s-\\t-$&sub/-" ↵
| GIT_INDEX_FILE=$GIT_INDEX_FILE.new ↵
git update-index --index-info ↵
&& mv "$GIT_INDEX_FILE.new" "$GIT_INDEX_FILE"' HEAD
```

This is adapted from an example in *git-filter-branch(1)*, but using Perl instead of *sed* for better portability (the original does not work with BSD-style *sed* commands, such as the one in OS X). It works by rewriting the output of git ls-files like so:

```
100644 6b1ad9fa764e36… 0       bar
100644 e69de29bb2d1d6… 0       foo/bar
```

which becomes:

```
100644 6b1ad9fa764e36… 0       sub/bar
100644 e69de29bb2d1d6… 0       sub/foo/bar
```

and updating the index accordingly for each commit. You can use this on a clone of the source repository in the git rebase recipe given earlier, to import one repository history into a subdirectory of another.

Updating Tags

In "Commit Surgery: git replace" on page 159, we said to use `git filter-branch` to apply object replacements made with `git replace` to the commit graph. There is a problem with this as given, though: it breaks any existing tags pointing to rewritten commits, since they remain untouched and continue to point to the old commits no longer on the rewritten branches. You can avoid this like so:

```
$ git filter-branch --tag-name-filter cat -- --all
```

Since `--tag-name-filter` rewrites tag names from stdin to stdout, cat acts as the identity filter and has Git rewrite all tags with their existing names unchanged as needed.

WARNING

This will strip GnuPG signatures from the rewritten tags and commits.

Notes

Keep in mind when importing history in these ways, that while Git preserves the author timestamps in rewritten commits, `git log` orders its output by the *commit* timestamps, which will be new. The new history may thus show commits in an unexpected order. This is correct though: the commit's content was created at one time, and that content was then committed to another repository at a later time. Unfortunately, `git log` does not have an option to order by author timestamp instead.

## CHAPTER 11

Understanding Patches

A "patch" is a compact representation of the differences between two files, intended for use with line-oriented text files. It describes how to turn one file into another, and is asymmetric: the patch from *file1* to *file2* is not the same as the patch for the other direction (it would say to delete and add opposite lines, as we will see). The patch format uses context as well as line numbers to locate differing file regions, so that a patch can often be applied to a somewhat earlier or later version of the first file than the one from which it was derived, as long as the applying program can still locate the context of the change.

The terms "patch" and "diff" are often used interchangeably, although there is a distinction, at least historically. A diff only need show the differences between two files, and can be quite minimal in doing so. A patch is an extension of a diff, augmented with further information such as context lines and filenames, which allow it to be applied more widely. These days, the Unix *diff* program can produce patches of various kinds.

Here's a simple patch, generated by `git diff`:

```
diff --git a/foo.c b/foo.c
index 30cfd169..8de130c2 100644
--- a/foo.c
+++ b/foo.c
@@ -1,5 +1,5 @@
 #include <string.h>
```

```
 int check (char *string) {
-      return !strcmp(string, "ok");
+      return (string != NULL) && !strcmp(string, "ok");
 }
```

Breaking this into sections:

```
diff --git a/foo.c b/foo.c
```

This is the Git diff header; diff --git isn't a literal command,
but rather just suggests the notion of a Git-specific diff in Unix
command style. *a/foo.c* and *b/foo.c* are the files being compared,
with added leading directory names *a* and *b* to distinguish them
in case they are the same (as they are here; this patch shows the
changes from one version to another of the same file). To generate
this patch, I changed the file *foo.c* and ran git diff, which shows
the unstaged changes between the working tree and the index.
There are in fact no directories named *a* and *b* in the repository;
they are just convention:

```
index 30cfd169..8de130c2 100644
```

This is an extended header line, one of several possible forms,
though there is only one in this patch. This line gives information
from the Git index regarding this file: 30cfd169 and 8de130c2 are
the blob IDs of the A and B versions of the file contents being
compared, and 100644 are the "mode bits," indicating that this is
a regular file: not executable and not a symbolic link (the use
of .. here between the blob IDs is just as a separator and has
nothing to do with its use in naming either sets of revs or for git
diff). Other header lines might indicate the old and new modes
if that had changed, old and new filenames if the file were being
renamed, etc.

The blob IDs are helpful if this patch is later applied by Git to the
same project and there are conflicts while applying it. If those
blobs are in the object database, then Git can use them to perform
a three-way merge with those two versions and the working copy,
to help you resolve the conflicts. The patch still makes sense to
other tools besides Git; they will just ignore this line and not be
able to use the extra information:

```
--- a/foo.c
+++ b/foo.c
```

This is the traditional "unified diff" header, again showing the files being compared and the direction of the changes, which will be shown later: minus signs will show lines in the A version but missing from the B version; and plus signs, lines missing in A but present in B. If the patch were of this file being added or deleted in its entirety, one of these would be /dev/null to signal that:

```
@@ -1,5 +1,5 @@
 #include <string.h>

 int check (char *string) {
-    return !strcmp(string, "ok");
+    return (string != NULL) && !strcmp(string, "ok");
 }
```

This is a difference section, or "hunk," of which there is just one in this diff. The line beginning with @@ indicates by line number and length the positions of this hunk in the A and B versions; here, the hunk starts at line 1 and extends for 5 lines in both versions. The subsequent lines beginning with a space are context: they appear as shown in both versions of the file. The lines beginning with minus and plus signs have the meanings just mentioned: this patch replaces a single line, fixing a common C bug whereby the program would crash if this function were passed a null pointer as its string argument.

A single patch file can contain the differences for any number of files, and git diff produces diffs for all altered files in the repository in a single patch (unlike the usual Unix diff command, which requires extra options to recursively process whole directory trees).

Applying Plain Diffs

If you save the output of git diff to a file (e.g., with git diff > foo.patch), you can apply it to the same or a similar version of the file elsewhere with git apply, or with other common tools that handle diff format, such as patch (although they won't be able to use any extra Git-specific information in the diff). This is useful for saving a set of uncommitted changes to apply to a different set of files, or for transmitting any set of changes to someone else who is not using Git.

You can use the output of git show *commit* as a patch representing the changes for a given nonmerge commit, as a shortcut for git diff *commit~ commit* (explicitly comparing a commit and its parent).

Patches with Commit Information

There is another patch format, specific to Git, that contains not only patches for some number of files, but also commit metadata: the author, timestamp, and message. This carries all the information needed to reapply the changes from one commit as a new commit elsewhere, and is useful for transmitting a commit when it is not possible or convenient to do so with the usual Git push/pull mechanism.

You produce this patch format with git format-patch, and apply it with git am. The patch itself is actually in the venerable Unix mailbox format, using the email "from," "date," and "subject" headers as the author, timestamp, and commit message subject, and the email body as the rest of the message. A commit patch for the previous example might look like this:

```
From ccadc07f2e22ed56c546951… Mon Sep 17 00:00:00 2001
From: "Richard E. Silverman" <res@oreilly.com>
Date: Mon, 11 Feb 2013 00:42:41 -0500
Subject: [PATCH] fix null-pointer bug in check()

It is truly a wonder that we continue to write
high-level application software in what is essentially
assembly language. We deserve all the segfaults we
get.

---
foo.c | 2 +-
1 file changed, 1 insertion(+), 1 deletion(-)
```

```
diff --git a/foo.c b/foo.c
...
```

The initial line contains the original commit ID, and a fixed timestamp meant to signal that this "email" was produced by git format-patch. The [PATCH] prefix in the subject is not part of the commit message, but rather intended to distinguish patches among other email messages. A diffstat summary of the patch comes next (which you can suppress with --no-stat (-p)), followed by the patch itself in the format shown earlier.

You run git format-patch like so:

$ git format-patch [*options*] [*revisions*]

The revisions argument can be any expression specifying a set of commits to format, as described in Chapter 8. As an exception, however, a single commit C means C..HEAD, i.e., the commits on the current branch not contained in C (if C is on this branch, these are the commits made since C). To get the other meaning instead —that is, all commits reachable from C—use the --root option.

By default, Git writes patches for the selected commits into sequentially numbered files in the current directory, with names reflecting the commit message subject lines like so:

```
0001-work-around-bug-with-DNS-KDC-location.patch
0002-use-DNS-realm-mapping-even-for-local-host.patch
0003-fix-AP_REQ-authenticator-bug.patch
0004-add-key-extraction-to-kadmin.patch
```

The leading numbers in the filenames makes it easy to apply these patches in order with git am *.patch, since the shell will sort them lexicographically when expanding the wildcard. You can give a different output directory with --output-directory (-o), or write the patches all to standard output with --stdout; git am reads from standard input if given no file arguments (or a single hyphen as the only argument, git am -).

git format-patch takes a number of other options for controlling the resulting email format, such as adding other mail headers, as well as many options taken by git diff to affect the diff itself; see *git-format-patch(1)* and *git-diff(1)* for more detail. Also see "Importing Linear History" on page 156 for some examples.

## CHAPTER 12

Remote Access

As mentioned in Chapter 6, Git can access remote repositories for push and pull using different network protocols; the most common are HTTP(S), SSH, and the native Git protocol. Especially if the remote repository accepts push requests, the access protocol may require you to identify yourself in order to grant access; this is called "authentication," and may be accomplished in various ways, such as by providing a username and password. The Git protocol does not support authentication, so this is usually done via HTTP or SSH; the native Git server, accessed on port 9418 with the URL scheme `git://`, is used almost exclusively for read-only access to repositories (for which it is a good choice, since it is fast and easy to set up).

The question of how to configure the server side for these protocols generally is well beyond the scope of this text; entire books have been written on SSH, the Apache web server, the Windows IIS web server, etc. However, we will touch on a few common cases from the client perspective, and on some Git features that help with this.

SSH

When you access a repository with a URL of the form:

```
[user@]host:path/to/repository
```

Git runs *ssh*, or the program given by the environment variable GIT_SSH, to log into the remote host and access the repository by running the appropriate remote command: git upload-pack for pull, and git receive-pack for push. The local and remote Git programs then communicate over the SSH channel to perform the requested operation. For example, when asked to pull from the repository dieter@sprockets.tv:dance/monkey, Git runs this command:

```
ssh dieter@sprockets.tv git-upload-pack dance/monkey
```

This logs into the host sprockets.tv with the username dieter, and runs the remote command git-upload-pack dance/monkey. If the host is Unix, usually this means that there must be a user account named dieter on that host, git-upload-pack must be in the program-search path on the remote side (the PATH environment variable), and the remote repository must be in a subdirectory of the dieter account's home directory named *dance/monkey*. You can refer to any directory to which the remote account has access by using a complete pathname with a leading slash (e.g., host:/var/lib/git/foo.git).

SSH will prompt you for a password if necessary, but it may be very inconvenient to do this repeatedly, so you may want some form of automatic authentication for this connection: a method by which you can type your passphrase just once and allow many subsequent Git commands. There are several different options for this, but the most common is SSH public-key authentication.

You can generate a new SSH public key thus if you don't already
have one:

```
$ ssh-keygen
Generating public/private rsa key pair.
Enter file in which to save the key (.ssh/id_rsa):
Enter passphrase (empty for no passphrase):
Enter same passphrase again:
Your identification has been saved in .ssh/id_rsa.
Your public key has been saved in .ssh/id_rsa.pub.
...
```

The "passphrase" is just another name for a password, empha-
sizing the fact that you can use an entire phrase with spaces and
punctuation, not just a single word. You should generally *not* just
leave this blank; that means that anyone who gets hold of the
private key file *id_rsa* will have access to any SSH accounts pro-
tected with this key. It's like putting your password in a file; don't
do it unless you really know what you're doing (or really don't
care about security).

You then send your public key—the contents of the file *~/.ssh/
id_rsa.pub*—to the server administrator, asking him to authorize
your key for login to the remote account; this usually means
placing it in *~/.ssh/authorized_keys* in the home directory of the

account, with appropriate ownership and permissions. When this is done, SSH will prompt you for the key passphrase instead:

```
$ git pull
Enter passphrase for key '/home/res/.ssh/id_rsa':
```

Enter your passphrase to test whether the setup is working correctly—though so far this is not much of an improvement in convenience; you're still being prompted to enter something for every Git command accessing the remote repository. The final step is to use the SSH "agent" to get automatic authentication:

```
# Test whether you have a running agent.
$ ssh-add -l >& /dev/null; [ $? = 2 ] && echo no-agent
no-agent
# If not, start one.
$ eval $(ssh-agent)
# Now, add your key to the agent.
$ ssh-add
Enter passphrase for /home/res/.ssh/id_rsa:
Identity added: /home/res/.ssh/id_rsa (.ssh/id_rsa)
```

On some modern Unix-based systems, you may not have to do any of this—for example, OS X starts an SSH agent for you when you log in, and SSH prompts you for your key passphrase with a graphical dialog box and automatically adds it to the agent on first use.

Once your key is loaded in the agent, you should be able to use Git to access this repository without giving your passphrase, for the duration of your current login session on the client computer.

You can also use this style of URL for SSH:

ssh://[user@]host/path/to/repository

A distinction to keep in mind is that, unlike the earlier style, the path given here is not relative to the remote account's home directory, but rather is absolute. You can get a relative path by prefixing the path with ~. For example:

ssh://host/~/path/under/homedir

although this may depend on the shell used by the remote account.

HTTP

A web server providing access to a Git repository may also be set to require authentication. Although more sophisticated mechanisms are available, including Kerberos and public-key certificates, the most common approach with HTTP is still to require a simple username and password. This complicates automatic authentication, but Git has its own framework for managing and providing such credentials.

Storing Your Username

You can include the username in an HTTP URL in the same way as with SSH:

```
https://dieter@sprockets.tv/...
```

But you can also set it separately, like so:

```
$ git config --global
credential.'https://sprockets.tv/'.username dieter
```

Storing Your Password

Git has a mechanism called "credential helpers," which stores passwords in various ways for more convenient use. One such helper, named `cache`, is similar to *ssh-agent* and caches your password in memory for use by Git. It is not used by default; to enable it, do:

```
$ git config --global credential.helper cache
```

Once you do this, Git should prompt you only once in a given login session for the password associated with any particular URL; when you provide it, Git stores it in the running credential cache agent, and subsequent commands automatically obtain it from there. If you look, you can see the agent process:

```
$ ps -e | grep git-cred | grep -v grep
33078 ttys001    0:00.01 ↵
git-credential-cache--daemon ↵
/home/res/.git-credential-cache/socket
```

Git communicates with the agent via the socket shown on the agent command line.

There is another standard credential helper named `store`, which simply stores the password in a file on disk (*~/.git-credentials*). You shouldn't do this for interactive use, but it is appropriate for automated processes that need to run Git and use password authentication, so long as adequate care is taken in protecting the host system and setting permissions on that file. You can also use the *cache* helper with automated processes if that level of security is not enough, but a human will have to enter the password once after the machine boots in order to add it to the cache, so this is not the right approach if the system in question must be able to start unattended.

The Git credential mechanism is extensible, and there are third-party helpers available that connect with platform-specific security features. For example, the helper `osxkeychain` stores passwords in the OS X "keychain," the standard credential manager for the Mac. It is included with the versions of Git installed by the Apple Xcode developer tools or by MacPorts (*http://www.macports.org/*). Just enable it with:

```
$ git config --global credential.helper osxkeychain
```

and it should work automagically. You can use the Keychain application to verify that Git is indeed storing its credentials there.

References

For more detail, see:

- *gitcredentials(7)*
- *git-credential-cache(1)*
- *git-credential-store(1)*

## CHAPTER 13

Miscellaneous

In this chapter, we cover some Git commands and topics that don't fit easily into any of the foregoing discussions.

git cherry-pick

`git cherry-pick` allows you to apply the changeset of a given commit as a new commit on the current branch, preserving the original author information and commit message. As a very general rule, it's best to avoid this in favor of factoring your work so that a commit appears in one place and is incorporated in multiple branches via merging instead, but that isn't always possible or practical. Any arrangement of branches and merge discipline favors a certain flow of changes, and sometimes you need to buck that flow. For example, you might discover that a bug fix applied to a certain version actually needs to be applied to an earlier one as well, and merging in that direction is not desirable. Or, suppose you have your own repository for holding local changes made to your Unix distribution's derivative of some open source project, such as Apache or OpenLDAP as modified and repackaged by Red Hat or Debian. If there is an upstream feature you need that the distribution does not provide (and they use Git), you can't just merge it in, as your repository is not a clone of theirs—but you may be able to apply the relevant commits individually by cherry-picking.

The argument to `git cherry-pick` is a set of commits to apply, using the syntax described in Chapter 8. Some options:

`--edit (-e)`
Edit the commit message before committing.

`-x`

Append to the commit message a line indicating the original commit. Only use this if that commit is publicly available; if you're cherry picking from a private branch, then this information is not useful to others.

`--mainline n (-m)`
For merge commits, compute the changeset for the new commit relative to the nth parent of the original. This is required to cherry pick merge commits at all, since otherwise it is not clear what set of changes should be replicated.

`--no-commit (-n)`
Apply the patch to the working tree and index, but do not commit. You can use this to take the commit's changes as a starting point for further work, or to squash the effect of several cherry picked commits into a single one.

`--stdin`
Take the commit list from standard input.

As with other commands that apply patches, `git cherry-pick` can fail if a patch does not apply cleanly, and it uses the merge machinery in that case, recording conflicts in the index and working files in the usual way. It then prompts you to use the options `--{continue,quit,abort}` to continue after resolving the conflicts, skip the current commit, or abort the whole cherry pick, similar to `git rebase`.

git notes

Since commits are immutable, you can't add to a commit message once you've made it (and you can't replace a commit you've pushed without causing woe for others). `git notes` provides a way to annotate commits for yourself later on while avoiding this difficulty.

The set of notes for your repository is maintained on a branch named `refs/notes/commits`, in the following fashion: to find the notes for a commit, Git looks up its 40-digit hex commit ID as a pathname in the tree of the current notes commit (tip of the *notes/ commits* branch); if present, that points to a blob that contains the text of the note. When you add or remove a note, Git simply commits the corresponding change to the notes branch (so you can see the history of your notes with `git log notes/commits`).

Though normally used to annotate commits, notes can in fact be attached to any Git object.

git notes Subcommands

You can use the `-f` option generally to override a complaint, such as to replace existing notes. A missing *object* argument defaults to HEAD, except where noted otherwise:

`git notes list [object]`
> List the notes for `object` by ID, or all notes with no `object`. A plain `git notes` invokes this subcommand.

`git notes {add,append,edit} [object]`
> Add a note for `object`, or edit or append to an existing note.

`git notes copy first second`
> Copy the note from one object to another.

`git notes show [object]`
> Display the note for `object`.

`git notes remove [object]`
> Delete the note for `object`.

You can specify a notes ref other than `notes/commits` with the `--ref` option; the argument is taken to be in `refs/notes` if unqualified. You can use this feature to have different categories of notes; perhaps notes on different subjects, or from different people (e.g., `git notes --ref=bugs`).

Initially, `git notes` seemed mostly geared toward private use; there was no explicit support for merging notes from other sources. Recent Git versions have added a `git notes merge` command, and this is improving; see *git-notes(1)* for the current status of that as well as other options.

git grep

`git grep` lets you search your repository content using regular expressions: not only the working tree, but also the index or any commit in the history without having to check it out. You can even use it outside a Git repository, as a more powerful version of the usual Unix *grep* command.

Combining Regular Expressions

Instead of a single regular expression, `git grep` can handle Boolean combinations of expressions, combined with the options `--{and,or,not}` in infix notation ("or" is the default connective; "and" binds more tightly than "or"; use parentheses for grouping, which you may have to escape to protect from your shell). In this usage, patterns are preceded by `-e`. For example:

```
$ git grep -e '^#define' ↵
--and \( -e AGE_MAX -e MAX_AGE \)
```

This finds lines that begin with #define and contain either AGE_MAX or MAX_AGE; thus, it finds both #define AGE_MAX and #define MAX_AGE.

NOTE

"Infix notation" means placing binary connectives between their arguments, rather than in front of them in function-call style; thus foo --and bar --or baz, rather than --and (foo (--or bar baz)).

What to Search

By default, `git grep` searches tracked files in the working tree, or given commit or tree objects. The given objects must be listed individually; you cannot use range expressions such as `master..topic`. You can add path limiters to restrict the files searched to those matching at least one glob-style pattern. For example:

```
$ git grep pattern HEAD~5 master -- '*.[ch]' README
```

Other options:

`--untracked`
> Include untracked files; add `--no-exclude-standard` to skip the usual "ignore" rules

`--cached`
> Search the index (that is, all blobs registered as files in the index)

`--no-index`
> Search the current directory even if it's not part of a Git repository; add `--exclude-standard` to honor the usual "ignore" rules

What to Show

By default, `git grep` shows all matching lines, annotated with filename and object as appropriate. Other options include:

`--invert-match (-v)`
> Show nonmatching lines instead

`-n`
> Show line numbers

`-h`
> Omit filenames

`--count (-c)`
> Show the number of lines that match, rather than the matching lines themselves

`--files-with-matches (-l)`
Just list the files containing matches

`--files-without-matches (-L)`
Just list the files containing no matches

`--full-name`
Show filenames relative to the working tree top, rather than the current directory

`--break`
Collate matches from the same file and print blank lines between resulting sets

`--heading`
Show the filename once before the matches in that file, rather than on each line

`--all-match`
With multiple patterns combined with "or," only show files that contain at least one line matching each pattern

How to Match

`-i (--regexp-ignore-case)`
Ignore case differences (e.g., hello and HELLO will both match "Hello").

`-E (--extended-regexp)`
Use extended regular expressions; the default type is basic.

`-F (--fixed-strings)`
Consider the limiting patterns as literal strings to be matched; that is, don't interpret them as regular expressions at all.

`--perl-regexp`
Use Perl-style regular expressions. This will not be available if Git is not built with the `--with-libpcre` option, which is not on by default.

git rev-parse

git rev-parse is a plumbing command, meant mainly for use by other Git programs to parse and interpret portions of Git command lines that use common options for specifying revisions. You can use it directly, though, and we've mentioned it before as a tool for showing what a given commit name spelling translates to. However, it also has several useful options for showing various properties of a repository, including:

--git-dir
  Show the Git directory for the current repository

--show-toplevel
  Show the top of the working tree

--is-inside-git-dir
  Indicate whether the current directory is inside the Git directory

--is-inside-working-tree
  Indicate whether the current directory is inside the working tree of a repository

--is-bare-repository
  Indicate whether the current repository is bare

git clean

git clean removes untracked files from the working tree, optionally limited by a glob pattern (e.g., git clean '*~' to remove backup files). Options include:

--force (-f)
  Really do something. git clean will make no changes without this flag, unless you set clean.requireForce to false.

--dry-run (-n)
  Show what would be done, but remove no files.

`--quiet (-q)`

    Report only errors, not the files removed.

`--exclude=`*pattern* `(-e)`

    Add `pattern` to the "ignore" rules in effect.

`-d`

    Remove untracked directories as well as files. Directories that are in turn other Git repositories will not be removed unless you add `-f -f` (two "force" flags).

`-x`

    Skip the normal "ignore" rules (but still obey rules given with `-e`).

`-X`

    Remove only ignored files.

There is no single `git clean` command that is most common, really; it depends on what you're trying to do. For example, often ignored files include compiled objects that are expensive to rebuild, so you don't want to remove them while cleaning up other untracked cruft that has accumulated in your working tree. On the other hand, after you switch branches, you may want to remove all object files to ensure a correct new build, as the dependencies in a complex project as expressed by tools like *make* or *ant* may not handle such wholesale rearranging of files correctly.

git stash

`git stash` saves your current index and working tree, then resets the working tree to match the HEAD commit as `git reset --hard` would do. This allows you to conveniently set aside and later restore your working state so that you can change branches, pull, or perform other operations that would be blocked by your current changes.

The saved states are arranged in a "stack," meaning that the last state you put into it is the first one you take out. That is: if you stash a state, make more changes, then stash again—when you next restore a state, it is the *second* state that is restored, not the first one. The terms "push" and "pop" used in the commands below are traditional in computer science for the operations of adding and removing something to and from a stack. Unlike a pure stack, however, the commands do generally allow you to bypass the stack order and directly address previous states, if you want to.

Subcommands

save

This is the default subcommand, saving the current working state as described. Options include:

`--patch (-p)`
> Interactively select hunks to save, rather than the complete diff between HEAD and the working tree. This works the same way as the patch mode of `git add`.

`--keep-index`
> Do not revert changes already applied to the index.

`--include-untracked (-u)`
> Save untracked files (normally only tracked files are saved). This is useful to save compilation artifacts such as object files, normally ignored and untracked but that would be costly to recreate.

You can also give a comment as an argument, to be saved as the message on the commit representing the stash (e.g., `git stash save "bugfix in progress"`). Otherwise, Git generates a default message like:

```
WIP on master: 72e25df0 'commit subject'
```

The `--keep-index` option is useful for testing partially staged changes before you commit them. If you use `git add -p` to split your current worktree changes into multiple commits ("Adding Partial Changes" on page 48), you may want to test those commits first. `git stash save --keep-index` preserves your staged changes and reverts the rest, so that you can test this intermediate state. You then commit, restore the remaining changes with `git stash pop`, and repeat.

list

List the stack of stashes, which can be referred to symbolically as `stash@{0}`, `stash@{1}`, and so on (most recent first). You can add options as to `git log`.

show

Show the changes in a given stash, as the diff between the stash and its corresponding original worktree state. The default is the latest stash (`stash@{0}`), and you can add options as with `git diff`.

pop

The inverse of `git stash`: restore a stashed state and remove it from the stash list; the default state to use is `stash@{0}`, or you can supply a different stash. If the stash does not apply cleanly, this does not remove the stash; use `git stash drop` after resolving the conflicts. With `--index`, restores the saved index as well (which is otherwise discarded).

apply

Like `git stash pop`, but does not remove the restored state from the stash list.

branch <branchname> [stash]

Switches to new branch starting at the original commit for `stash`, and restores the stash there. This is useful when the working tree has changed such that the stash no longer applies cleanly.

drop [stash]

Remove `stash` from the stash list (default `stash@{0}`).

clear

Deletes the entire stash list.

git show

`git show` displays a given object (default HEAD) in a manner appropriate to the object type:

commit
> Commit ID, author, date, and diff

tag
> Tag message and tagged object

tree
> Pathnames in (one level of) the tree

blob
> Contents

For example, to see the diff from one commit to the next, you could use `git diff foo~ foo`, but `git show foo` is just simpler. The command takes any options valid for `git diff-tree` to control display of the diff, including `-s` to suppress the diff and just show the commit metadata. You can also use `--format` as described in "Defining Your Own Formats" on page 130 to customize the output.

git tag

A Git tag gives a stable, human-readable name to a commit, such as "version-1.0" or "release/2012-08-01". There are two kinds of tags:

- A "lightweight tag" is just a ref in `refs/tags` pointing to the tagged commit.

- An "annotated tag" is also a ref in `refs/tags`, but pointing to a tag-type object instead, which in turn not only points to the tagged commit, but records other information as well: the tag author, timestamp, a tag message, and an optional GnuPG cryptographic signature.

`git tag` *tagname* *commit* creates a new lightweight tag pointing to the given commit (default HEAD). Options include:

`--annotate` (`-a`)
> Make an annotated tag instead

`--sign` (`-s`)
> Make a signed tag (implies `-a`), using the GnuPG key for the committer's email address or the value of `user.signingkey`

`--local-user=`*key-ID* (`-u`)
> Make a signed tag (implies `-a`), using the specified GnuPG key

`--force` (`-f`)
> Be willing to replace existing tags (this normally fails)

`--delete` (`-d`)
> Delete a tag

`--verify` (`-v`)
> Verify the GnuPG signature on a tag

`--list` *pattern* (`-l`)
> List tags with names matching `pattern`. No pattern means list all tags, and this is the default for a plain `git tag` command without arguments. Multiple patterns means to list tags matching at least one pattern.

`--contains` *commit*
> List tags containing the given commit; that is, those that have `commit` as an ancestor of the tagged commit

`--points-at` *object*
> List tags that point to the given object

`--message="text"` (`-m`)
> Use text as the tag message (instead of invoking the editor). Multiple `-m` options are concatenated as paragraphs. This implies an annotated tag.

```
--file=filename (-F)
```
> Use the contents of `filename` as the tag message (instead of invoking the editor); "-" means standard input. This implies an annotated tag.

Deleting a Tag from a Remote

Deleting a tag from your repository will not automatically delete it from the origin when pushing; you have to do that explicitly:

```
$ git push origin :tagname
```

Following Tags

When you pull (or fetch) from a configured remote, Git will automatically fetch new tags, but a "one-shot" pull specifying the remote repository (`git pull URL branch`) will not do this. This rule tries to match the likely desires of people in the given situation. If you are collaborating closely with a set of people on a project, you are likely to want to share tags with them, and also likely to be using the push/pull mechanism with a configured remote. On the other hand, if you have to specify the other repository, then you probably aren't collaborating closely over that particular content, and so you probably don't want to automatically pull in the other group's tags.

In any case, `git pull` never automatically overwrites tags. A tag can represent sensitive assertions about the tagged commit, such as its being a certain official release of a product, or containing an important security fix. Once accepted, a tag should not silently change without the user knowing. If you push out a botched tag, the preferred way to fix it is to simply use a new tag name. Actually updating an already pushed tag is awkward, by design. See the "DISCUSSION" section of *git-tag(1)* for more detail.

For new tags you create, use `git push --tags` to send them when pushing.

Backdating Tags

You can set the tag date with the `GIT_COMMITTER_DATE` environment variable. For example:

```
$ GIT_COMMITTER_DATE="2013-02-04 07:37" git tag…
```

git diff

`git diff` is a versatile command, showing the difference between content pairs in the working tree, commits, or index. The following are some common forms.

git diff

This shows your *unstaged* changes; that is, the difference between the working tree and the index.

git diff --staged

This shows your *staged* changes; that is, the difference between the latest commit and the index. These are the changes that will be included in the next commit. `--cached` is a synonym for `--staged`. You can give an alternate commit to compare as an argument; the default is HEAD.

git diff <commit>

This shows the difference between the working tree and the named commit.

git diff <A> <B>

This shows the difference between two commits, trees, or blobs A and B. `A..B` is a synonym for `A B`; note that this has no connection to the meaning of that syntax when naming sets of commits (see "Naming Sets of Commits" on page 123). If either A or B is omitted in `A..B`, the default is HEAD; this syntax is thus useful for specifying HEAD for one of these by just typing two dots, which is easier and faster than typing in all caps.

Options and Arguments

You can limit the comparison to specific files with trailing patterns; for example, this shows the unstaged changes only in Java and C source files:

```
$ git diff -- '*.java' '*.[ch]'
```

git diff accepts quite a few options controlling how Git computes or displays differences, most of which it has in common with git log, which we discuss in Chapter 9. For example, this summarizes the differences instead of displaying them:

```
$ git diff --stat
 foo.c     | 1 +
 icky.java | 1 +
 3 files changed, 3 insertions(+)
```

and this just lists the files that contain differences:

```
$ git diff --name-only
foo.c
icky.java
```

git instaweb

Git comes with a web-based repository browser called "gitweb." Setting up a standalone web server to provide general access to a set of Git repositories is outside our scope here; however, Git has a convenience command git instaweb that starts a special-purpose web server giving *gitweb* access to the current repository. Just start it with:

```
$ git instaweb --start
```

and point your browser at *http://localhost:1234/* (assuming your browser is running on the same host; otherwise, use the right hostname). Use --port to select a different TCP port, and --stop to stop the gitweb server when you're done.

If you type just git instaweb, it will start or restart the gitweb server, and then launch a browser from the command line on the same host. This may not be what you want; you might be logged into that host remotely without any way to display graphics from it (e.g., a local X Windows server combined with SSH X forwarding), and so Git will end up starting a character-based browser such as *lynx*.

By default, this command uses the `lighttpd` web server, which must also be installed. It supports several other web servers as well, including Apache, which you can select with `--httpd`; see *git-instaweb(1)* for details.

Git Hooks

In computer jargon, a "hook" is a general means of inserting custom actions at a certain point in a program's behavior, without having to modify the source code of the program itself. For example, the text editor Emacs has many "hooks" that allow you to supply your own code to be run whenever Emacs opens a file, saves a buffer, begins writing an email message, etc. Similarly, Git provides hooks that let you add your own actions to be run at key points. Each repository has its own set of hooks, implemented as programs in *.git/hooks*; a hook is run if the corresponding program file exists and is executable. Hooks are often shell scripts, but they can be any executable file. `git init` automatically copies a number of sample hooks into the new repository it creates, which you can use as a starting point. These are named *hookname.sample*; rename one removing the *.sample* extension to enable it. The sample hooks themselves are part of your Git installation, typically under */usr/share/git-core/templates/hooks*. The *templates* directory also contains a few other things copied into new repositories, such as the default *.git/info/exclude* file.

For example, there is a hook named `commit-msg`, which is run by `git commit` after the user edits his commit message but before actually making the commit. The hook gets the commit message in a file as an argument, and can edit the file in place to vet or alter the message. If the hook exists with a nonzero status, Git cancels the commit, so you can use this to suggest a certain style of commit message. It's only a suggestion though, because the user can avoid hook with `git commit --no-verify`; it's his repository, after all. You'd need a different kind of hook on the receiving end of a push to enforce your style on a shared repository.

The *githooks(5)* man pages describes in detail all the different hooks you can use, and how they work.

Visual Tools

Complex commit graphs, file differences, and merge conflicts are best viewed graphically, and there are a number of tools available for this. Git itself includes *gitk*, which is written with the Tcl/Tk language and graphics toolkit, as well as the simple `git log --graph`. Here are some other useful tools in this category:

tig (https://github.com/jonas/tig)
> A terminal-based tool using the "curses" library.

QGit (https://sourceforge.net/projects/qgit/)
> Using the QT4 GUI framework, QGit builds and runs essentially identically on multiple platforms, including Linux, OS X, and Windows.

GitHub (https://github.com/)
> There is a GitHub application for OS X, Windows, and the Eclipse programming environment. It can work with your own repositories as well as with ones hosted on the GitHub service.

SmartGit (http://www.syntevo.com/smartgithg/index.html)
> SmartGit runs on Linux, OS X, and Windows, and works with the Mercurial version control system as well.

Gitbox (http://gitboxapp.com/)
> Specific to OS X with a very nice, native Mac look and feel.

Submodules

Sometimes, you need to use the source to another project in yours, but it is not possible or appropriate to combine the two into a single repository. This situation can be awkward to handle. You may not want to keep merging the entire history of another project into yours, where it will clutter up your own history (though the "subtree" merge strategy can be helpful if you decide to do this).

Git has a feature called "submodules" to address this: it allows you to maintain another Git repository as a tracked object within a subdirectory of yours. In the tree of a commit in your repository, the submodule reference includes a commit ID in the foreign repository, indicating a particular state of that repository. This defines the content of the corresponding directory for your commit, while still leaving all its refs and objects out of your repository proper.

As an advanced feature, we do not discuss submodules further here; see *git-submodule(1)* for details.

## CHAPTER 14

How Do I…?

This final chapter presents some commands and recipes for accomplishing a grab bag of specific tasks. Some were presented earlier and are repeated or referred to here for easy reference, and some are new. Remember that you don't usually want to edit history for commits you've already published with `git push`. Examples that refer to a remote repository use the most common case, `origin`. `rev` is any revision name as described in Chapter 8.

…Make and Use a Central Repository?

Suppose you have an account named `ares` on a server `mars.example.com`, which you want to use to coordinate your own work on a project `foo` (perhaps among repositories at home, work, and on your laptop). First, log into the server and create a "bare" repository (which you will not use directly):

```
$ ssh ares@mars.example.com
ares> git init --bare foo
Initialized empty Git repository in /u/ares/foo/.git
$ logout
```

If this is for a project with existing content, connect that repository to the new remote as its origin (assuming here a single, local *master* branch):

```
$ cd foo
$ git remote add origin ares@mars.example.com:foo
```

```
$ git push -u origin master
...
To ares@mars.example.com:foo
* [new branch]      master -> master
Branch master set up to track remote branch master
from foo.
```

You can just use plain `git push` from then on. To clone this repository elsewhere:

```
$ git clone ares@mars.example.com:foo
```

...Fix the Last Commit I Made?

Make your corrections and stage them with `git add`, then:

```
$ git commit --amend
```

Add `-a` to automatically stage all changes to tracked files (skipping `git add`). Add `-C HEAD` to reuse the previous commit message without stopping to edit it.

See "Changing the Last Commit" on page 58.

...Edit the Previous n Commits?

```
$ git rebase -i HEAD~n
```

The history involved should be linear. You can add `-p` to preserve merge commits, but this can get tricky depending on the changes you want to make.

See "Editing a Series of Commits" on page 64.

...Undo My Last n Commits?

```
$ git reset HEAD~n
```

This removes the last *n* commits of a linear history from the current branch, leaving the corresponding changes in your working files. You can add `--hard` to make the working tree reflect the new branch tip, but beware: this will also discard any current uncommitted changes, which you will lose with no recourse. See

"Discarding Any Number of Commits" on page 61. This will also work if there is a merge commit in the range, effectively undoing the merge for this branch; see Chapter 8 to understand how to interpret HEAD~*n* in this case.

…Reuse the Message from an Existing Commit?

```
$ git commit --reset-author -C rev
```

Add --edit to edit the message before committing.

…Reapply an Existing Commit from Another Branch?

```
$ git cherry-pick rev
```

If the commit is in a different local repository, ~/other:

```
$ git --git-dir ~/other/.git format-patch ↵
-1 --stdout rev | git am
```

See:

- "Importing Linear History" on page 156
- "git cherry-pick" on page 181

…List Files with Conflicts when Merging?

git status shows these as part of its report, but to just list their names:

```
$ git diff --name-only --diff-filter=U
```

…Get a Summary of My Branches?

- List local branches: git branch

- List all branches: `git branch -a`
- Get a compact summary of local branches and status with respect to their upstream counterparts: `git branch -vv`
- Get detail about the remote as well: `git remote show origin` (or other named remote)

See "Notes" on page 91.

...Get a Summary of My Working Tree and Index State?

    $ git status

Add `-sb` for a more compact listing; see the "Short Format" section of *git-status(1)* on how to interpret this.

...Stage All the Current Changes to My Working Files?

    $ git add -A

This does `git add` for every changed, new, and deleted file in your working tree. Add `--force` to include normally ignored files; you might do this when adding a new release to a "vendor branch," which tracks updates to other projects you obtain by means other than Git (e.g., tarballs).

...Show the Changes to My Working Files?

`git diff` shows unstaged changes; add `--stage` to see staged changes instead. Add `--name-only` or `--name-status` for a more compact listing.

...Save and Restore My Working Tree and Index Changes?

git stash saves and sets your outstanding changes aside, so you can perform other operations that might be blocked by them, such as checking out a different branch. You can restore your changes later with git stash pop. See "git stash" on page 188.

...Add a Downstream Branch Without Checking It Out?

```
$ git branch foo origin/foo
```

This adds a local branch and sets up push/pull tracking as if you had done git checkout foo, but does not do the checkout or change your current branch.

...List the Files in a Specific Commit?

```
$ git ls-tree -r --name-only rev
```

This listing is restricted to the current directory; add --full-tree for a complete list.

...Show the Changes Made by a Commit?

git show rev is easier that git diff rev~ rev, and shows the author, timestamp, commit ID, and message as well. Add -s to suppress the diff and just see the latter information; use --name-status or --stat to summarize the changes. It also works for merge commits, showing conflicts from the merge as with git log --cc (see "Showing Diffs" on page 142). The default for rev is HEAD.

...Get Tab Completion of Branch Names, Tags, and So On?

Git comes with a completion package for *bash* and *zsh*, installed in its git-core directory as git-completion.bash. You can use it by including (or "sourcing") this file in your shell startup file (e.g., in ~/.bashrc):

```
# define completion for Git
gitcomp=/usr/share/git-core/git-completion.bash
[ -r $gitcomp ] && source $gitcomp
```

Pressing Tab in the middle of a Git command will then show possible completions for the given context. For example, if you type git checkout, space, and then press Tab, the shell will print the branches and tag names you could use here. If you type an initial part of one of these names, pressing Tab again will complete it for you. The exact behavior of completion is very customizable; see your shell man page for details.

There is also a git-prompt.sh, which will make your shell prompt reflect the current branch status when your working directory is a Git repository.

...List All Remotes?

git remote does this; add -v to see the corresponding URLs configured for push and pull (ordinarily the same):

```
$ git remote -v
origin  http://olympus.example.com/aphrodite (fetch)
origin  http://olympus.example.com/aphrodite (push)
```

...Change the URL for a Remote?

```
$ git remote set-url remote URL
```

...Remove Old Remote-Tracking Branches?

```
$ git remote prune origin
```

This removes tracking for remote branches that have been deleted upstream.

...Have git log:

Find Commits I Made but Lost?

...perhaps after editing history with `git rebase -i` or `git reset`, or deleting a branch:

```
$ git log -g
```

See "Double Oops!" on page 59.

Not Show the diffs for Root Commits?

A root commit always shows the addition of all the files in its tree, which can be a large and uninformative list; you can suppress this with:

```
$ git config [--global] log.showroot false
```

Show the Changes for Each Commit?

`git log -p` shows the complete patch for each commit it lists, while these options summarize the changes in different ways:

```
$ git log --name-status
$ git log --stat
```

See "Listing Changed Files" on page 136.

Show the Committer as well as the Author?

```
$ git log --format=fuller
```

Index

We'd like to hear your suggestions for improving our indexes. Send email to index@oreilly.com.

The information you need, when and where you need it.

With Safari Books Online, you can:

Access the contents of thousands of technology and business books

- Quickly search over 7000 books and certification guides
- Download whole books or chapters in PDF format, at no extra cost, to print or read on the go
- Copy and paste code
- Save up to 35% on O'Reilly print books
- **New!** Access mobile-friendly books directly from cell phones and mobile devices

Stay up-to-date on emerging topics before the books are published

- Get on-demand access to evolving manuscripts.
- Interact directly with authors of upcoming books

Explore thousands of hours of video on technology and design topics

- Learn from expert video tutorials
- Watch and replay recorded conference sessions

O'REILLY®

Milton Keynes UK
Ingram Content Group UK Ltd.
UKHW011039260824
447358UK00002B/8

9 781449 325862